trade
IPOs
online

Wiley Online Trading for a Living

Electronic Day Trading to Win / Bob Baird and Craig McBurney

The Strategic Electronic Day Trader / Robert Deel

Day Trade Online / Christopher A. Farrell

Trade Options Online / George A. Fontanills

Electronic Day Trading 101 / Sunny J. Harris

Trade Stocks Online / Mark L. Larson

How I Trade for a Living / Gary Smith

Day Trade Futures Online / Larry Williams

Trade IPOs Online / Matthew D. Zito and Matt Olejarczyk

trade
IPOs
online

MATTHEW D. ZITO

MATT OLEJARCZYK

John Wiley & Sons, Inc.
New York · Chichester · Weinheim · Brisbane · Singapore · Toronto

Library of Congress Cataloging-in-Publication Data:

Zito, Matt, 1969–
    Trade IPOs online / Matt Zito & Matt Olejarczyk.
       p. cm. — (Wiley online trading for a living)
    ISBN 0-471-38474-7 (cloth : alk. paper)
      1. Going public (Securities) 2. Investments. I. Olejarczyk, Matt, 1970–
II. Title. III. Series.

HG4028.S7 Z57 2000
332.63′223—dc21

                                          00-021720

Printed in the United States of America.

10 9 8 7 6 5 4 3 2 1

foreword

This is truly a glorious time to be alive and have money for investments in the stock market. I have been on Wall Street for over 23 years, spending the past 10 as president of IPOfinancial.com. In structuring a company that broke down the walls of closely held information about IPOs and delivered this quantitative analysis to institutions, hedge funds, brokers, and individuals, I never dreamed of a market that would embrace a stock like Netscape that went public in 1995 at $28 and opened at $72.75. The Microsofts and Apple Computers of the 1980s have had their molds not only shattered but recast for the new generation of Internet IPOs. A "hot listed" IPO in our system was a stock that we expected to open with a ½ point price premium over the IPO price. Nowadays, if a stock opens with a 5-point premium, it is considered to be a failure and is at risk of being viciously sold off and going below its IPO price. Insane you say? Of course, when the average investor has seen opening premiums of 50, 100, and 200+ points at the very first trade.

It is senseless to list the best opening performances for IPOs because few of you probably got any of those IPO shares. That is the number one nagging question we get from our subscribers and registrants to our site: "How can I get into the IPOs at the IPO price and not have to chase these stocks at the opening of trading when they open at treetop tall prices?" The answer is simple, but the question is an acknowledgment that the average investor just doesn't know the rules. Traditional business, up until a few years ago, was dictated solely by what type of a trading profile you showed both the broker and the brokerage firm. Quid pro quo at its finest. You scratch my back (commissions generated for the broker) and I'll scratch yours (IPO allocations for the customer—maybe).

That system is so political that it has turned many people off IPOs. That is how the general climate of the IPO market has turned to cynicism. Why bother trying if all the stock goes to the big money investors, right? WRONG!

Enter the online IPO brokerage community. Through the pioneering work of firms like Wit Capital, the wall on Wall Street has started to look like the crumbling Berlin Wall. The individual has been heard and is getting greater allocations of IPOs than ever before. The online community has created a new paradigm in the IPO brokerage community. Expect the online firms to cast a larger and larger shadow over the traditional "good ole boy" network that is the mainstay of the IPO market—the full-service brokerage firm. Their grip will weaken as individual investors exercise more power through their current friend in the SEC, Arthur Levitt. The Internet may be the white knight for the IPO business.

But we need to ask an important question: Why are you even thinking about IPOs—new companies that are financially unseasoned and very high risk—instead of the stocks that have a long string of quarterly results and analysts following them? The answer is simple. More millionaires have been made in the IPO market than any other segment of the stock market. In fact, you could even go so far as to say more billionaires have been made in IPOs than any other segment of the market. More media attention has been given to IPOs, especially Internet IPOs, than at any other time in modern history, more people, more issues, more shares, more this, higher that, better everything. The world of Internet IPOs is all about superlatives.

Conventional wisdom has taught many of us in the stock market about successful investment strategies that encompass the rock-solid approach of long-term capital gains. When you go into a full-service brokerage firm to open an account, you generally get muscled around in the new account interview—the most intimidating phase of doing business with the brokerage community. Your prospective broker, who is attempting to get to know you (not because he cares that much, but rather to comply with the "know your customer" rule), fires question after question at you. In the interview process, you are asked that all important question, "What are your investment objectives?" The answer you give—or in many cases, the answer you are guided to—will directly affect what securities the compliance department will let you trade.

Time to put on the ol' Stars-and-Stripes underwear and vote for the American free-enterprise system. "Let's invest in America!" You need to help the companies of this great country by letting the entrepreneurs run with their ideas. Again we go back to the age-old wisdom of our investment forefathers—long-term capital appreciation—a great and admirable trading objective. Let's check that box on the new account form. Hey, wait a minute, does that qualify you for buying IPOs? Sure, because these new companies are in need of capital to "grow" their companies and, as we all have been taught, that takes time—even years—to achieve. Your broker has told you that if you check short-term trading profits, you would not be considered for any IPOs because that is not what IPOs are all about. Does that mean that when an IPO doubles, triples, or even more at the opening that you can't sell it? Not at all, but you may step on some people's toes in the process. IPOs are very much about long- and short-term trading. The only thing you have to learn is which hat to wear and when.

Never has a concept like the online IPO market taken such a strong foothold in the very foundation of the investment community. With the online IPO brokerage community come the Internet IPO resources for more information, commentary, and analysis than ever thought possible. An area of the Internet that will apparently always have great promise is the compilation and organization of the millions of mega- and terabytes of information now at our disposal. Many sectors of business reduce their collective wisdom to three words. In real estate, they are "location, location, and location." In the IPO market, they are "timing, timing, and timing." But whatever business you are in, the one common thread is that information is power. In this book, you will find out how to get it and then how to use it for profit.

DAVID MENLOW
President, IPOfinancial.com

preface

Are you taking full advantage of the new opportunities to buy initial public offerings? How can you profit from the opportunity to buy at the offering price?

Use the newest and greatest developments in online investing to your benefit. Learn from the IPOguys, Matt Olejarczyk and Matt Zito, who have succeeded in the IPO market and can teach you how to invest in it.

Together, the IPOguys strategically purchased, and helped many others purchase, some of the hottest IPOs of 1999 including CBS Marketwatch.com (MKTW), purchased at $17/share and sold at $95⅛ per share; Healtheon/Web-Med (HLTH), purchased at $8.00/share, then sold at $46⅜ per share; Vertical Net (VERT), purchased at $16/share, then sold a majority stake at $46/share, and the rest at $143/share; Wit Capital Group, purchased at $9.00/share, then sold a majority stake between $24–$25. The preceding highlights are just a few of the many IPOs purchased by the IPOguys. In just the first half of 1999, they successfully purchased IPOs in more than 35 companies.

Matt Zito is an entrepreneur, individual investor, and trader. He is cofounder of the IPOguys.com financial based Web site, and coauthor of this book *Trade IPOs Online*. He is President and CEO of Ski & Sand Travel, Inc., and Skisavers.com, one of the leading collegiate Ski & Snowboard Tour companies in America. Matt is also co-owner of the Yellow Breeches House Fly-Fishing Lodge in south central Pennsylvania. Matt Zito has been featured in the *Wall Street Journal, Home Office Computing* magazine, and the *Washington Post.* Matt has been investing since he was 22 years old. He stays busy trading IPOs, writing for the IPOguys.com Web site, and spending time with his wife, Nicole, and their Golden Retriever, "Sir Charles of the Yellow Breeches," aka "Monks."

Matt Olejarczyk is an individual investor, IPO trader and analyst, and data specialist. He is cofounder of the IPOguys.com financial based Web site, and coauthor of *Trade IPOs Online*. He is also the Founder of Oley Enterprises, which is dedicated to assisting in the personal well-being and financial growth of individuals. Matt has been investing since he was 21 years old. He spends most of his time researching, tracking, and trading IPOs online. He also writes for the IPOguys.com Web site, which is committed to helping the individual investor obtain access to IPOs at the offering price.

The IPOguys believe that investors can become millionaires by investing in IPOs. Over their 18 years of combined investing experience, they have never found any other investment vehicle that can produce gains even remotely comparable to those of IPOs.

Not only do the IPOguys believe in the future of IPOs in the hands of the individual investor, they see the future of business in America, and of our global economy, as resting heavily on the new information-based economy. They put their money where their mouth is by primarily trading IPOs online and investing in today's market of information and technology.

About This Book

The information in this book is not just "book-smart" IPO investing, but is very much about "street-smart" investing, taken from our personal experiences purchasing and selling IPOs online.

The first goal of this book is to teach you how to make money investing in IPOs, to help you organize and simplify your research, and to minimize the time you take to make profitable IPO investing decisions. After all, the most important thing for the individual investor to do is to get started investing in IPOs.

The information in this book, combined with a little common sense, is all you will need to quickly begin purchasing IPOs. Many people successfully purchase their first IPO in just two weeks.

Our second goal for this book is to provide practical information about this brave new world of IPO investing. Countless revisions have gone into the attempt to include essential facts and differing perspectives that will help readers become highly successful IPO traders.

We have identified useful tools, strategies, and information sources available to the IPO investor, including the prospectus, a detailed review of current Web sites dedicated to IPO investing, and a review of some leading publications that focus on the technology and the Internet sectors. We also take a look at the venture capitalist, in addition to some of the leading IPO analysts, and discuss how they can help guide the IPO investor along the way.

Research into IPO investments will take you to the forefront of the Internet revolution. As an individual investor, you will acquire a knowledge base from researching and investing in IPOs that should carry forward to other investment vehicles. Investing in IPOs may make you a better investor in the long term by broadening your comprehension of the entire investment community.

We still invest in blue chip stocks, and mutual funds, but have steadily increased the percentage of our total portfolio targeted for buying IPOs. Individual investors are discovering that IPOs are truly a "new investment vehicle" and are gaining greater access to this once closely guarded financial opportunity. The advantage still favors the wealthy and institutional investor, but we anticipate a larger percentage of the IPO allocation being sold and distributed to knowledgeable individual investors. We hope this book will help prepare you, the individual investor, for the coming increased access to IPOs.

IPO investing can be a powerful strategy to achieve significant wealth. It has worked for us, and it can work for you. We wish you the best in your endeavor to obtain increased financial independence by profiting from the lucrative world of IPO investments.

Best Wishes, and Freakin' Hit It,

MATTHEW D. ZITO
MATT OLEJARCZYK
"The IPOguys"

acknowledgments

From Matt Zito

Writing this book has required hard work, organization, and a focus on the positive events and experiences in my life that have contributed to its creation. Many friends, family members, and mentors have come to mind during this undertaking.

First and foremost, I thank my beautiful wife, Nicole, for sticking by my side from the beginning and putting up with all my entrepreneurial adventures. My mother and father inspired me as a youngster to never give up. Their discipline and guidance have helped me prosper throughout my life. To my sister, thanks for creating the IPOguy image; you are a talented artist. To the Zito, Farber, Haskins, and Puglisi families for always being there on special family outings; to the newest addition to our family the Jergensens; to my adventurous mother- and father-in-law, truly creative and giving. Thanks also to Mike Devlin, Judy Slonaker, and Thomas Pestke at Boyer & Ritter Certified Public Accountants, and Michael Hund of Reed Smith Shaw & McClay LLP.

I also want to acknowledge my friends John, Elaine, and Marty Laughbaum; Roger Shapiro, "aka Trigger"; Maureen O. Driscoll (Daren would have loved this); Trent, Sally, and Sydney Dudley; Jannette Esguerra; John and Val Kiracofe; the Carlisle CC boys; the Fairview High gang; the Murray family; the Betas of 9-201. Finally, to Robert Conley, wherever you are: the university classes you taught inspired me to shoot for the moon.

Jan Rumberger and Steve Schoffstall introduced me to the venture capital and Internet world. Bobby Glass and the crew at Acorn

Financial Services helped my wife and me get started in our financial and entrepreneurial lives. Thank you all.

From Matt Olejarczyk

Our original motivation for this book came, not from a publishing deal, but from our initial encounter with a single IPO. Once we experienced firsthand the incredible returns that are achievable in IPO investing, we knew we had to share this opportunity with our families and close friends. Soon, we were spending more time answering questions and helping others buy IPOs than we were affording ourselves the luxury commonly referred to as "sleep." That is when we decided to leverage our time by organizing our notes into a logical sequence for others to read and learn from. So the first version of this book was written, and the rest is history.

The readers of the early manuscripts, especially my brother Paul, my Uncle Steve, Jeff Klein, and Dr. Jennifer Murphy, provided excellent questions and feedback that challenged us to improve the quality of information in this book. I also wish to thank all of my teachers and mentors, both in school and in life, and my colleagues, especially "the doc" Dr. Craig Sponseller, Martin S. Tendler, Keith Sheppelman, Roger Schulenberg, Steve Miller, Dr. John Coyle, and Dr. Robert Novack. And to all of my friends and family, thank you for being there to share these great life experiences.

Most importantly, I thank my family, to whom I owe every success. Thank you Dad for teaching me the value of hard work and responsibility, and for being such a great role model. Thank you Mom for raising me in a home full of love and support. And last but not least, thank you and bless you Gram for your spiritual inspiration and guidance. I am fortunate and blessed. You can't place a value on the impact of a supportive family, friends, or a positive thought.

Special Thanks

The following entrepreneurs, analysts, online investment banks, Web media companies, and academia contributed to this work by granting interviews, answering questionnaires and e-mails, editing the manuscript, and reading proofs: David Menlow from the

IPO Financial Network; Tom Taulli, Scott Ryles, Rob Zimmer of RadioWallStreet; Francis Gaskins, John Fitzgibbon from Redherring; Larry Kramer from CBS Marketwatch.com; Corey Ostman from Ostman's Alert-IPO.com; Ben Holmes of ipopros.com; Kenan Pollack and Lisa Glass from Hoovers.com; Jay Sears from EDGAR-Online.com; Diane Carlson from Business 2.0; John DeFalco of ipo-data.com; Irv DeGraw, Jay Ritter, Ivo Welch, Ryan Ballow, and Eric Wedbush from einvestmentbank.com; Eric Brugal of FBR.com; Rhee Rosenman from Wit Capital Group; Sharon Smith from WR Hambrecht + Co.; and Jennifer Cross of E*OFFERING.

In addition, we thank Larry Connors of TradingMarkets.com for referring our manuscript to John Wiley & Sons, and Pamela van Giessen, our editor, for helping us share this great new investment vehicle with the online individual investor.

M. D. Z
M. O.

contents

introduction

Matt Zito

It all started one day during the fall of 1998 in the offices of the Software Colony in Camp Hill, Pennsylvania. I was there pitching my newest brain trust idea—Skisavers.com—looking for venture start-up capital to fund my fledgling Internet company. It was my second appointment with Jan Rumberger, one of the founders of the Software Colony, and he had invited a well-known entrepreneur in the south central Pennsylvania area, Steve Schoffstall, to meet me. Steve was a cofounder of PSInet, one of the largest Internet service providers in the country. Steve, who had recently moved to south central Pennsylvania after cashing out of PSInet, was looking for his next Internet adventure.

We all hit it off, and for the next two months, I met with Steve regularly for lunch to explain my progress with Skisavers.com. During these meetings, I learned the inside process that Internet companies go through in raising capital prior to going public. The entire process (I'll call it "the game") was unlike anything I had ever experienced before; it was an eye-opening introduction to high-tech Internet life.

My wife, Nicole, and I had started two successful companies before, but we had never raised capital from outside sources, especially venture capitalists. Over the next 3 to 6 months, I developed the business plan for Skisavers.com, researched the competitors, and talked to potential clients. I soon discovered that two companies in Silicon Valley were already developing the same technology I had envisioned. I also soon learned that ski resorts, my main source of revenue, were reluctant to have anything to do with the Internet, let alone pay a start-up for something they thought they could do themselves. The ski resorts didn't want to spend a dime.

As the game continued and I furthered my research, I fell upon a Web site called Red Herring (redherring.com). I was researching venture capital resources and saw a banner ad for Wit Capital that read something like "wanna be like a venture capitalist" "buy ipos online." I thought "wow," what an opportunity. I knew what an initial public offering was because the development of Skisavers.com was intended to lead to an IPO that would be the "pot of gold" at the end: the company would turn public raising millions of dollars. Today, many Internet entrepreneurs are becoming millionaires and billionaires through taking their companies public.

My wife and I have been investing since we were 22 years old, mainly in mutual funds and big blue chip stocks. I had never heard of an avenue for investing in IPOs the way the venture capitalists do. Like most people, I thought this "party" was limited to investors with $1 million or more. I visited the Web site and saw that Wit Capital was offering to sell "initial shares" in many Internet companies that were coming public. The companies going public were similar to what I was trying to build in Skisavers.com. My wife and I decided to open an account at witcapital.com.

While I was developing Skisavers.com, Matt Olejarczyk, a colleague and friend, had showed an interest in starting his own business. Shortly thereafter, he started sharing some of his ideas for Skisavers.com. I would send him my business plan, and he would review it for me. I then told him about how I had set up an account with witcapital.com. After following a few companies on paper (paper trading), he became convinced that there was a huge opportunity to invest in initial public offerings. Because Olejarczyk put a lot of time into researching and developing software and Internet utilities that would help us gain an edge over other potential IPO investors, we were successful in obtaining shares in more IPOs than we knew what to do with. We had gone from standing ankle-deep on the water's edge to diving headfirst into the IPO ocean. We thought we had better take advantage of this incredible new investment opportunity while we still could. Little did we know, it was only the beginning.

It was January 14, 1999, around 7:30 P.M., and we both had just received reconfirmation e-mails from Wit Capital for a new issue named Marketwatch.com (CBS Marketwatch). We had read the prospectus a few weeks earlier, researched the company through various IPO Web sites, and decided we were going to try to buy 100 shares of the new issue at $17.00 a share. Total cost for 100 shares was $1,700.00.

A lot of positive hype surrounded the company, and the technology market was booming. We both reconfirmed our original conditional offer for 100 shares of Marketwatch.com. That evening we were extremely excited because we knew that the shares would start trading the next day a lot higher than our original $17.00 a share purchase. I don't think we slept real well that night; in fact, I know I didn't because I got up around 4:30 A.M. to see whether I had received an allocation.

I went to the computer, logged in, and downloaded my e-mail. There it was, an e-mail from Wit Capital; the words in the subject header read "NewIssueAlertMKTW." I knew the e-mail was something important—at least I hoped so—considering that I hadn't slept all night in anticipation of this very moment. As I clicked on the message, I saw that I had in fact been allocated 100 shares in MKTW (CBS Marketwatch.com). Figure I.1 shows a sample e-mail confirmation.

I talked with Matt Olejarczyk that morning, and sure enough he also had been allocated shares in Marketwatch.com. Matt was so excited I am pretty sure he dedicated his entire morning to sitting in front of the computer just so he could see what the stock would start trading at that morning.

About 11:30 A.M. the next day (Friday, January 15), my wife and I were coming back from the hardware store with supplies to

Figure I.1 E-mail Confirmation

Dear Matt Zito:

Wit Capital hereby accepts your conditional offer in the amount of 100 shares of Marketwatch.com Inc. Common Stock. The offering has been priced at $17.00 per share.

Trade date: 1/5/99

Settlement date: 1/20/99

Symbol: MKTW

You will receive a confirmation by mail containing further details of this trade.

Source: Sample e-mail confirmation from Wit Capital. Used with permission.

fix up our fly-fishing lodge. The cell phone rang and it was my mother-in law, Irene. She could barely speak, but she finally got it out, "Matt, Marketwatch is trading at $92.00 a share." I was stunned. We had just paid $17.00 a share the night before, and now it was trading at $92.00 a share.

Nicole first said, "Let's sell it. I don't think we have ever made $7,500.00 in less than 24 hours on 100 shares of a stock." Although we decided not to sell that day, we did end up selling half of our initial 100-share investment, 50 shares, at $81.50 a share five days later. That was a profit of $3,225.00 in less than 5 days (50 shares of the IPO only cost $850.00). This was exciting.

CBS Marketwatch.com ended up number six on the all-time list of first-day performers during the 1999 calendar year, with a first-day gain of 474 percent. Even though we were thrilled beyond belief that day, we realized that the run would not last. Not every IPO was going to go up 474 percent.

To make money investing in and trading IPOs online, we were going to have to make it our business. Investing in IPOs takes discipline and commitment. You must take the time to do your homework, and also realize that you cannot gain significant wealth overnight. So Matt Olejarczyk began researching software and technology that would help us to obtain IPOs at the offering.

Together, we have participated in the purchase of over 35 IPOs in 1999. A majority of the new issues have been winners, big winners, while a few IPOs have not fared as well. Yet overall, we have never seen such a consistently lucrative investing opportunity. Trading IPOs does not guarantee a profit. This investment vehicle is extremely volatile over the short term, and highly risky over the long term. But IPO investing is like anything else in life; when you seek high returns, you must also accept a higher level of risk. Matt and I also believe, however, that hard work, commitment, and dedication can offset much of the risk in this endeavor.

I hope we got your blood pumping, or at least piqued interest in initial public offerings. Maybe you have already heard enough about IPOs to know that you want to know more. Either way, you're ready to get started.

We are going to take you through the same process we followed in learning how to trade IPOs. The first, and probably the most important, step as you begin your IPO investing journey, is to build a solid foundation. In Chapter 1, we describe how the Internet has spawned a whirlwind of change in the investing and financial industries. This will help you understand how the Internet created an opportunity for the individual investor to obtain IPO shares at the offering price. We refer to these changes, and time frame surrounding them, as the "Internet Investing Revolution."

After you understand the events that created this new opportunity for the individual investor to obtain shares at the offering price, we begin to discuss the IPO in detail. In Chapter 2, then, we cover the capital formation process and discuss IPOs as a new investment vehicle.

Once you know how the IPO typically performs in the market, you will have greater success in your investing and trading strategies. Therefore, in Chapter 3 we look at IPO performance. In Chapter 4, we detail specifically the Internet IPO and show you why the best current IPO investing opportunities lie in Internet-related IPOs.

Every IPO investor will appreciate Chapter 5, probably even more so after you begin trading IPOs and can look back at it in hindsight. In Chapter 5, we recommend preinvesting research and preparations for anyone who even considers getting involved in trading IPOs online. In Chapter 6, we get to the heart of actual IPO investing. Here we walk you through the process, from setting up an account to deciding what trading strategies to use once you've been allocated shares.

Once you know how to set up an online account, then you need to find out where to open one. In Chapter 7, we highlight which online investment banks currently sell IPOs to individual investors so you can decide where to take your money. Next, in Chapter 8, we provide insight on leveraging software and information technology to assist in the purchase of IPOs online. Finally, in Chapter 9 we discuss the future of IPOs and online individual investing.

The IPOguy fights for access to IPOs for the individual investor. The IPOguy is a knowledgeable, responsible, shrewd, and dedicated individual investor. True to his entrepreneurial spirit, he takes his investment decisions seriously.

The IPO is a new investment vehicle for the individual investor. Access is now open. The IPOguy is willing and ready to take you on a journey that will demystify any previous notions you may have had about IPOs. We hope this journey will increase your knowledge about the possibilities for trading or investing in IPOs.

The IPOguy will pop up throughout this book. He should not be taken lightly. Wherever he makes an appearance, please take special note.

The IPOguy welcomes you in the fight for access to the coveted IPO.

Now it is time to HIT IT!

chapter 1

the internet
investing revolution

A revolution is taking place . . . right now . . . in front of our very eyes, just beyond the thousands of pulsating light pixels per square inch on our computer monitors. Commonly referred to as the "information revolution," the Internet will directly or indirectly impact every aspect of our lives. Whether it's a new technology that transmits data faster than ever before, or a consumer-based Web site that sells products at 20 percent to 40 percent below traditional "brick and mortar" stores, the Internet Revolution will affect you as a consumer in one way or another. And like the industrial revolution, this new revolution will change our lives forever.

We use the term "revolution" because it most accurately reflects the incredible rate of change that is taking place in the financial world as a result of the Internet. Over the past couple of years, the world has embraced the Internet as an efficient and effective means to organize and make available high-quality investing information to the general public. Take a look for yourself. A wealth of information is available on the Internet to facilitate smart investment decisions, and much of it is the same information used by professional brokers.

Expert Information

Historically, the traditional brokerage firm's primary value has been expert investment decisions that result from having access to quality information not readily available to the general public. With the Internet, however, the individual investor is armed with just as much quality information as the "experts." The Internet takes that information power and places it in the hands of the individual investor. This has been the primary reason for the growth of online brokerage accounts.

The Individual Investor

Having high-quality financial information available over the Internet has allowed people to better understand their investments, track their investments, do their own stock analysis, and develop their own investing strategies.

Enter the scene online brokerage firms that allow people to perform stock trades online, at a much lower cost than that charged by traditional brokerage firms. It makes sense. Why pay a broker an enormous commission for research and trade execution, when you can research and execute the trade yourself, at a fraction of the cost?

The result is that individuals are taking responsibility for their financial situation and investing for themselves. People are using the Internet as their expert information source and are no longer willing to let a broker handle all their investments. Persons who invest a portion of their money for themselves over the Internet are referred to as an "online individual investor."

The Shift to Online Investment Accounts

Many people have opened online investment account(s) hoping to make returns that equal or exceed those of a broker. How many have opened accounts so far? "The percentage of U.S. investors trading online is now about 12.5 percent and is expected to climb to 29.2 percent by 2002. About 12 million of those households now have online accounts, and those folks are making more than a half-million trades a day."[1]

If those statistics don't boggle your mind, try these: "A June survey by Gomez Advisors, Inc., a Lincoln, Massachusetts, Internet research firm, and Harris Interactive Inc., A Rochester, New York, market-research firm, found that 4.6 million online investors had traded at least once in the prior 6 months. And despite fears of a slowdown in online trading activity, the survey found that 16.3 million more people were poised to begin trading online."[2]

This is not a fad, but a revolution that will change the face of investing forever. And this is just the beginning. E-commerce is expected to reach over 1.3 trillion dollars before the end of 2003. It is estimated 100,000 new Internet accounts are opened every day, and the number of online accounts doubles every 60 days.

Our aim here is to avoid getting hung up on numbers, because they are always changing. If we focused only on the numbers, we would have to revise this page of the book every 60 days or so because that is how fast the estimates seem to change. Our goal here is simply to give you some facts and figures that reveal the significance of the revolution taking place in our homes via our computers.

Impact on Traditional Brokerage Firms

Traditional brokerage firms such as Morgan Stanley Dean Witter, Fidelity, and most recently Merrill Lynch (to name a few) have noted this phenomenon and jumped online, or developed software aimed at the individual investor, in an attempt to garner a portion of this ever-growing market. An educated, online investor is the reality of the future, and a growing portion of the individual's discretionary income will be allocated to these online accounts, most likely at the expense of traditional brokerage firms.

The Motivation of the Individual Investor

"Making the Big Score"

The lure of making it big has always drawn people to drastic measures. For example, during the California Gold Rush of 1848–1849 fortune seekers from all over the country traveled West hoping to strike it rich. America's fascination with gambling is another example. According to some analysts, gambling addictions have reached epic proportions. Casinos in Las Vegas and elsewhere lure countless hopefuls through their doors, and there seems to be no sign of a deteriorating market. In fact, the latest battle has been how to keep gambling offline. If people actually believe they will win money consistently at the casinos, then why would they not believe that they have better odds at making a fortune by investing for themselves?

If you have a gambling habit, beware! You should not, in any way, confuse individual investing with gambling. Investing your hard-earned dollars in the stock market is not even remotely related to gambling. Sure you could pick any old stock by rolling the dice, and hope for a winner. But this book is not about getting lucky. It is about careful planning and smart investing in new market opportunities. Our culture's preoccupation with money can easily blur the lines between "investing" and "gambling" for many people.

Bad Experiences with Past Brokers

Another reason some people have taken to investing for themselves is that they have had bad experiences with a broker. Either they lost some money in their investments, or maybe they just watched their money make a nominal return while the rest of the market reached record highs. Maybe this has happened, or is still happening, to you.

Or maybe you just want to become a little more involved in managing your money, because, let's face it, no one cares as much about your money as you do. So you are going to open an online account. Whether you inform your other broker that you are doing some individual investing needs to be your personal decision. Only you know how good your relationship is with your broker. Keeping them "in the loop" on your personal investing activities could be mutually beneficial. However, when it comes to your broker losing some of your money to an online trading account, relationships tend to go sour. That has been our experience anyway.

Most of the brokers from the traditional firms have advised us against any sort of online personal investing activities. If I could have a dollar for every time a traditional broker advised me to "stay away" from online trading, or told me that I was "gambling," I could feed myself for at least a couple of weeks. "You're gambling,"— that's my favorite. If you have never been hit with that one yet, consider yourself lucky.

Some individual brokers at the traditional brokerage firms have been sheltered from understanding the impact of the online financial revolution and they just don't "get it" yet. Other brokers, who understand all too well the dramatic effect that the Internet is having on the investing public, will advise you against any involvement in it and tell you to leave it up to the "professionals."

We hope you will find this is more often the exception than the norm, although our personal experience has proven the reverse true. But we remain optimistic that in the long term, the traditional brokerage firms will survive and thrive through the chaos, and will continue play a critical role in the financial and investing sectors. Our vote is for developing educated and informed investors, not for leaving investors in the dark. While there are many brokers who will do a decent job for you, you will never find a broker who is as committed about your investments and your financial future as you are.

The reality today is that you need to take individual responsibility for your investments, whether you let a full-service brokerage firm handle your investments, or decide to do it on your own, or more likely combine both strategies. You never know when you have a second-rate broker until it is too late. So it is important that you take responsibility and at a minimum learn basic "investing talk." When you can intelligently discuss your investments with your broker, you can start making the most out of your hard-earned nest egg. Further, you may have more peace of mind knowing that your investments are "in synch" with your investment objectives.

Expectations and Objectives

The motivation to open an individual account is not always based on a bad experience. Maybe your expectations are just a little different from those of a traditional brokerage firm, perhaps a little higher than what is considered to be the standard. Table 1.1 shows a standard, textbook risk versus return chart that summarizes the average return by traditional investment type.

This table may be representative of what the "average" investor is able to achieve. But the individual investor does not settle for average results. Instead, we use the newest developments and strategies in the area of personal investing to outperform the averages. We will discuss one such strategy, trading IPOs online, beginning in Chapter 2.

Improved Control

The online trading tools and resources that are in place enable the online individual investor to make informed investing decisions and see immediate results. No longer do you have to leave a voice mail with a broker that you want to trade a stock, then hope that the transaction maximizes your profit. Or watch your stock tumble due to a recent news announcement while you wait on hold for your broker, who is on the other line. No longer do you need to guess where you rank on your broker's priority list of clients. You can place your market order and, within seconds, view your completed transaction. Controlling the money that you worked so hard to earn brings a level of satisfaction and independence that can only be understood by the online individual investor.

Table 1.1   IPO Classic Long-Term Risk versus Return

Investment Type	Expected Long-Term Performance (%)		
	Low	Average	High
Low-risk (bonds/CDs)	3	5	7
Medium-risk (stock funds)	2	10	18
High-risk (single stocks)	−10	14	32

Time Restrictions

Last but not least, you need to carefully consider the time factor. Some people simply don't have the time required to do their own investing. Make no mistake about it, to succeed in the world of investing, you need to be able to dedicate time to this endeavor.

If you have enough time to do some research and want to take more responsibility for your financial future, an individual online investment account might be just the thing for you. If you already have your own individual investment account, or if you plan on opening one in the near future, we are going to show you how to make money through your individual investment account by investing in IPOs.

Summary

- The Internet is shaking up the financial community by arming the individual investor with quality financial information, empowering us to make our own investing decisions. People are realizing the importance of taking responsibility for their financial future and becoming more actively involved in their investment decisions.

- It is important that you take responsibility for your financial future by actively participating in your investment decisions. Whether you invest for yourself or have someone else invest on your behalf, your level of involvement and investing knowledge will directly affect your financial success. One of the new and unique investing vehicles available to the online individual investor is the IPO.

chapter 2

ipos, the new investment vehicle

Everywhere you look today, whether in the *Wall Street Journal,* or *Money Magazine,* or on CNBC, the acronym IPO seems to pop up. IPO is the buzzword in both the high-tech world and the investment community.

In this chapter, we will discuss the IPO, the new investment vehicle, describe the players involved in launching an IPO, and look at each of their roles in the process. We will also try to demystify the truth about IPO investing and the impact it can have on the total return in your investment portfolio.

So, what is an IPO? IPO is an abbreviation for "initial public offering" and refers to the issue and sale of a stock to the public for the first time. In the early stages of development, young, private enterprises issue and sell stock to raise capital for expansion and growth.

With the increased speed at which business operates today, small private companies must obtain large amounts of capital (money) quickly in order to compete. To raise these huge sums, the company sells ownership positions in the form of equity *stock* or *debt bonds.* A stock is an equity investment that represents partial ownership in a company. A bond is an equity investment that represents ownership of a portion of debt to be repaid with interest to the bondholder by the company.

Although requiring capital to support future expansion and growth is the primary reason that companies go public, this may or may not mean that the funds raised will be used to build a new factory, hire more staff, or support ongoing research and innovation. The company is free to use the capital as it sees fit. Often some of the money is used to pay off outstanding debt.

The Capital Formation Process

When a company seeks to raise capital via an initial public offering, the entire procedure is known as the "capital formation process." In addition to the issuing company, many key players are involved during this process: the investment bank (also known as the lead underwriter, or managing underwriter), the syndicate (additional underwriters), the Securities Exchange Commission (SEC), the institutional investors, and now two brand-new players, online investment banks and the online individual investor.

The Investment Bank—A Traditional Player

A company that decides to go public usually hires an underwriter, also known as the lead underwriter or the managing underwriter. The main business of the underwriter during the capital formation process is to buy shares from the issuing companies, and then sell the shares to the public. Underwriting is the business of buying the original shares from companies going public, and controlling the resale and distribution to the investing public. The underwriting process is mutually beneficial and equitable for the companies going public and the investment banks. The investment banks provide an invaluable service of raising tremendous amounts of capital for the cash-hungry emerging companies. The cash-hungry companies benefit because their financial needs are fulfilled. The majority of the risk sits heavily on the shoulders of the investment banks initially, to create demand by promoting and then selling the existing shares to the public. Underwriting is the primary business of investment banking, although investment banks are involved in other activities such as mergers and acquisitions.

The Syndicate—A Traditional Player

To spread out this risk and to appeal to a larger investing base, multiple underwriters are often involved in the same deal. The syndicate is a distribution network of investment banks that work collectively to underwrite an initial public offering while reducing the risk associated with the underwriting process. Figure 2.1 shows an example of a typical syndicate, as found in a *Wall Street Journal* advertisement.

The Securities Exchange Commission—A Traditional Player

The Securities Exchange Commission (SEC) is the governing agency responsible for overseeing the issue of new securities and enforcing the Securities Act of 1933. The SEC's main function focuses heavily on protecting the investors within the United States; the agency makes sure that all securities information is open and reported accurately and fairly to investors. Private companies seeking to conduct an initial public offering must file a "registration statement" with the SEC. This statement, also known as the S-1, is a lengthy document containing pertinent facts about the firm planning to sell new securities. Facts contained in the registration statement include core business, key management personnel, and operational and financial information. Once the SEC determines the issuing company has fully disclosed all the relevant details of the offering, it will declare the registration statement effective.

Another important document required by the SEC is called the prospectus. The prospectus is a condensed version of the registration statement that details a new issue security (or IPO). The prospectus provides potential investors with a complete analysis of the potential risks associated with investing in the registered company. A preliminary version of the prospectus, also known as the red herring, is the same document as the prospectus except that it does not contain price information or the offering date. The document gets its nickname from the red ink on the first page that states the document is not an official offer to sell securities.

The Institutional Investor—A Traditional Player

Traditionally, institutional investors were the sole clients of investment banks. Institutional investors are generally large public

Figure 2.1   Wall Street Journal Ad—Medscape

This announcement is neither an offer to sell, nor a solicitation of an offer to buy, any of these securities. The offer is made only by the Prospectus.

November 17, 1999

7,650,000 Shares

Common Stock

Price $8.00 Per Share

Copies of the Prospectus may be offered in any State from such of the undersigned as may legally offer these securities in compliance with the securities laws of such State

Donaldson, Lufkin & Jenrette

Credit Suisse First Boston

Bear, Stearns & Co. Inc.

Wit Capital Corporation

DLJ*direct* Inc.

Deutsche Banc Alex. Brown	Goldman, Sachs & Co.	Hambrecht & Quist
ING Barings Lehman Brothers	Merrill Lynch & Co.	J.P. Morgan & Co.
Robertson Stephens	Salomon Smith Barney	SG Cowen
George K. Baum & Company	Doft & Co., Inc.	First Union Securities, Inc.
Gruntal & Co., L.L.C.	HCFP/Brenner Securities	Janney Montgomery Scott LLC
McDonald Investments Inc.	Needham & Company, Inc.	Punk, Ziegel & Company
Raymond James & Associates, Inc.	Sanders Morris Mundy	Sands Brothers & Co., Ltd.
SunTrust Equitable Securities	Sutro & Co. Incorporated	Tucker Anthony Cleary Gull
C.E. Unterberg, Towbin	Volpe Brown Whelan & Company	B.C. Ziegler and Company

Source: Wall Street Journal. Used with permission.

or private entities such as local governments, state governments, universities and colleges, other banks, mutual funds, and wealthy families. Investors with over $1,000,000 in equity can also be deemed an institutional investor. In addition to selling IPOs to institutional investors, investment banks also sell other traditional brokerage products and services. Because institutional investors have the liquidity to buy thousands of shares, they are ideal clients for the investment banking industry.

The Online Investment Bank—A New Player

The online investment bank is a new entity in the world of investment banking. Online investment banks are being formed because an increasing number of online individual investors are moving to control their own finances. The advent of the online investment banks has already created a complete shakeup of the traditional investment industry and ultimately will reshape the investment banking industry's traditional rules and practices. Online investment banks clients primarily are the individual investors. In addition to offering electronic trading services, some online investment banks offer "initial shares" in initial public offerings to their online clients.

The Online Individual Investor—A New Player

The online individual investor is a responsible, knowledgeable, and empowered investor. Online investors are any individuals who have made an effort to take control of their investment future— entrepreneurs, corporate employees, homemakers, social workers, computer technicians, engineers, mechanics, stock clerks, government workers, and salespeople. As a group, online individual investors one day will be larger than any institutional investor in the world.

Online individual investors are the main clients for the new wave of online investment banks. Online individual investors can research, buy, and sell from anywhere in the world. They can make decisions on their own time and will not be dictated to, but are free to call the shots and do anything, in any way, that they choose. Online individual investors will rule the future of financing in America.

The History of the Capital Formation Process

Historically, private companies have used investment banks to raise capital and manage the underwriting process. The other roles and responsibilities previously listed have remained unchanged for almost a century. So why is it now, only with the introduction of the Internet into the equation, are new key players being introduced into the game? To understand and appreciate how this list of key players came about, it is helpful to look back at the history of the capital formation process in the United States.

Investment banks in the early 1900s were developed to bring together the formation of capital. They came into play and became prevalent during the industrial revolution when steel and machinery companies needed money for growth and expansion. These banks acted as middleman between the larger financial institutions and the steel and machinery companies seeking capital. Much of the money raised by those early investment banks here in the United States came from large financial banks in Europe. The industrial revolution spawned what today are some of the biggest investment banks in the world.

Control of Distribution, and Scarcity

In the earlier days, the investment banks could control the selling of the shares to the public by selling shares when they wanted to. The investment banks controlled the number of shares sold, and at what price. The investment banks pretty much had complete control over the distribution and allocation process. By controlling the distribution, they could create demand through scarcity. Basic economics tells us that a combination of high demand and low supply means higher prices. A supply of only two thousand of those automobiles built back in 1964 means you will pay dearly for the collectible automobile you want today. The existence of only a few diamonds of a particular cut and clarity equals a high price for that engagement ring. The ultimate example of scarcity, only one Mark McGuire home run number 70 baseball, means almost an assured one million dollars or more for the person who caught it. The law of scarcity also applies to stocks. Three million new issue shares being offered to potential investors, and demand for 20 million shares, means a rapid rise in price when the stock starts trading. This may sound absurd, but we have owned a few Internet IPOs where the demand exceeded supply by as much as thirty to one. Scarcity in supply coupled with high demand ultimately leads to share price increases when the stock is sold to the public. A good underwriter will use its network to help create a high demand for an initial public offering, thereby creating a level of scarcity that will ensure a new issue will increase or at least maintain its price once it starts trading on the open market.

Today's Blue Sky Laws

Today, underwriters still control the distribution of shares, but they do not have complete freedom in the distribution of shares as in the past. Stringent guidelines imposed by the SEC surround the issuance and distribution of shares. These guidelines protect investors from receiving overly positive descriptions of companies, similar to a "blue sky." The SEC requires companies to file a wide range of documents that accurately and fairly disclose all potential risks to investors. The prospectus, however, is the primary document targeted toward ensuring all potential risks are disclosed to investors. The prospectus is discussed in detail in Chapter 5 since it is probably the single most important document used by the IPO investor.

Distribution of IPO Shares

In addition to having to complete required documentation, companies distributing shares follow a strict procedure as set forth by the SEC. Once the SEC has all documentation and approves the registration statement, the underwriter(s) and the company must agree on a price at which to sell the shares to investors who have previously expressed interest. The SEC declares the registration statement "effective," the price is set, and investors are informed that they can participate in an IPO at the set price. The price is usually established the day before the shares will begin trading, although there are exceptions to this timing on occasion, and shares might be priced on the same day that they begin trading. The SEC has helped establish standard guidelines by which investors must reaffirm their conditional offer in the offering. These guidelines have changed with the introduction of online investment banks into the equation, and we anticipate they will evolve over time. Once the conditional offer has been reaffirmed, the shares are then distributed to investors.

Most of the time, shares are allocated to investors the same day the final price is determined, usually in the evening after the market closes for the day. Once the shares have been distributed, they will begin trading in the secondary market the following day. This timing is typical of almost every IPO, although it may vary depending on special circumstances. In Chapter 6, we will guide you through a step-by-step procedure of placing a conditional offer to buy an IPO all the way through the reaffirmation and allocation process of the IPO.

Underwriting Fees and Commission

Investment banks underwriting a deal make money by buying the shares of the issuing company going public and reselling the shares to their clients, the institutional investors, at a higher price. The difference between the price paid by the investment bank for the shares and the selling price at which it offers the shares to clients is called the "gross spread," or the "underwriter's discount and commission." Basically, the underwriter buys at one price, then quickly turns around and sells at a higher price. The Multex.com initial public offering shown in Table 2.1 is a sample of the prices paid and the proceeds to each of the parties involved.

The table reveals that the issuing company sold the shares to the underwriter at a discount of $0.98/share, or $13.02/share. The

Table 2.1   Proceeds and Fees from an Initial Public Offering

	Per Share	Total
Issue Price	$14.00	$42,000,000
Underwriting Discounts and Commissions	0.98	2,940,000
Proceeds to Multex.com (the Underwriter Price)	$13.02	$39,060,000

underwriter resold the shares to the institutional investor at the higher price of $14.00/share. Multex.com raised $39,060,000 as a result of the initial public offering. The underwriter got paid commission of $2,940,000, or 7 percent of the total proceeds raised. The commissions paid to underwriters generally range between 4 percent and 8 percent of the total proceeds, with the average being closest to 7 percent.

Underwriting within the Syndicate

The lead manager will underwrite the majority of shares, followed by the comanager or comanagers. The other investment banks in the syndicate will underwrite smaller numbers of shares. The shares underwritten by all the underwriters will sum up to the total number of shares being offered in the deal. In the case of Multex.com, there were 3,000,000 total shares. Table 2.2 shows that there were 17 members in the syndicate, who underwrote varying numbers of shares.

Overallotment or "Green Shoe"

One of the advantages to being the lead underwriter, besides the opportunity to control the shares, is a coveted option called the overallotment. The overallotment is also known as the "green shoe" in the investment banking industry. The overallotment is a negotiated option by the investment bank to buy a second allocation or a larger amount over and above the original issuing amount. The investment bank generally negotiates for the right to buy 10 percent to 15 percent more than the total amount issued. If the investment bank exercises the overallotment allocation of say 15 percent, then the

Table 2.2   Syndicate Underwriting

Underwriter	Shares
BancBoston Robertson Stephens Inc.	1,132,500
CIBC Oppenheimer Corp.	566,250
Dain Rauscher Wessels	566,250
Goldman, Sachs & Co.	60,000
Gruntal & Co., LLC	60,000
Merrill Lynch, Pierce, Fenner & Smith	60,000
US Bancorp Piper Jaffray Inc.	60,000
Salomon Smith Barney Inc.	60,000
SG Cowen Securities Corporation	60,000
Wit Capital Corporation	60,000
George K Baum & Company	45,000
JC Bradford & Co.	45,000
E*TRADE Securities	45,000
Legg Mason Wood Walker, Inc.	45,000
Raymond James & Associates, Inc.	45,000
Volpe Brown Whelan & Company, LLC	45,000
Wedbush Morgan Securities Inc.	45,000

investment bank will buy 750,000 more shares. While the investment banks are out talking to the institutional investors about buying the shares, they can determine how much demand there will be. If it looks as if there will be great demand for the new issue, the lead manager will try to negotiate the right for overallotment.

Misconceptions Surrounding IPOs

IPOs are probably the most misunderstood investment vehicles that exist. Many investors may never have even heard the term IPO, or if they have, cannot accurately define it. Even today, with all the quality financial information available on the Internet, a great majority of the investing community still does not know, in any level of detail, what an IPO is, much less how it can turn a profit.

See for yourself. Make a few phone calls and see how many of your friends or associates know anything about IPOs. Ask the following questions: Do you know what an IPO is? Could you explain it to me? Have you ever bought an IPO? Did you buy it before it started trading on the stock market, or on the first day, or did you wait a while? Could I buy an IPO before it starts trading on the open market?

You probably will find that a majority of your acquaintances know very little if anything, about IPOs. This should prove to you that you are on the leading edge of something that is not widely known, often misunderstood, and very big.

New Issue Price (Offering Price) versus Market Price

There is a major difference between buying an IPO at the new issue (offering) price prior to the first day of trading, and buying the IPO at market price on or after the first day of trading in the secondary market. IPOs have always been available to the individual investor on the first day of trading, in the secondary market. However, only in the past year or two have IPOs been available to the individual investor at the new issue price, or the offering price.

Understanding the difference between buying the IPO at the offering price versus buying on the secondary market is critical. The profit potential is great and the risks are greatly reduced when you buy an IPO at the offering price compared with buying on the aftermarket on the first day of trading.

For now, we only mention the profit potential and risk reduction so that you clearly distinguish between buying IPOs at the offering price and buying them in the secondary market right from the start. If you are intrigued at the difference in profit and risk between buying IPOs at the offering price and buying IPOs on the open market, we cover the details of IPO performance in Chapter 3. For the remainder of this book, when we refer to buying IPOs, we are referring to buying them at the offering price.

IPOs—The New Investment Vehicle

Another misconception surrounding the IPO is that it is impossible for the individual investor to obtain shares at the offering price. This is plain and simply no longer true. The Internet has rendered this assumption false! Online investment banks have broken the tradition of offering shares in the hottest IPOs only to the wealthy and are helping to provide the retail investor access to these shares. This is only the beginning. It is easy to understand why there is such a misunderstanding surrounding IPOs. If you are one of the many frustrated individuals who have unsuccessfully tried to purchase IPOs prior to the open market, then you know exactly what we are talking about. Historically, it has been next to impossible to get any shares at the new issue price, so why bother? Why dangle the carrot right in front of your nose if you can never take a bite?

Although IPOs were traditionally available only to large institutions and wealthy individuals, the Internet has revolutionized the financial community and has opened the door for online individual investors like you and me. Today, we can purchase IPOs at the offering price via the Internet through online brokers or online investment banks. So get ready to go ahead and take a bite of that carrot.

The Internet has broken down the traditional walls to this prized investment opportunity. You may have heard of the standard 80/20 rule that is applied to modern business. This rule also applies to wealth in the United States. It is said that 80 percent of U.S. wealth belongs to 20 percent of the population. This is the same 20 percent who in the past have had access to purchasing IPOs at the offering price.

You may reasonably argue that the majority of the IPO shares are still allocated to the institutional investors and to the extremely wealthy. This is true. However, there are plenty of good IPOs out there to be bought at the offering price by prepared online individual investors who know what they are doing. By the time you finish this book, you may be one of those prepared IPO investors ready to claim your IPO shares.

As individual online investors gain increasing allocations of IPOs, large institutions and wealthy individuals are reaping a smaller percentage of them. The rules are changing and the online individual investor is benefiting. The increased allocation of IPOs to individual investors has caused a stir among institutional investors over the past year or more, although the American press has only recently started reporting on this trend. One headline we found about the competition for IPOs was in the *Wall Street Journal*,

"Now, Big Institutional Investors Gripe Over IPO Allocations, Too."[1] The demand for Internet and technology IPOs amplifies this battle over the highly sought-after IPO.

Efficiencies in IPO Allocation and Distribution

Why are individual investors only now gaining access to IPOs? The answer, in a word, is the Internet. New issues, or IPOs, at the offering price can now be sold or distributed to investors in a very short period of time. The Internet has created one of the fastest distribution processes in the history of our country. In less than one minute, online brokers and investment banks can e-mail thousands of potential investors about upcoming investment opportunities. What traditionally took weeks or even months in the past now can be accomplished in a matter of days (see Figure 2.2).

Figure 2.2   The IPO Mountain. Individual Investors are working their way up to the top of the mountain.

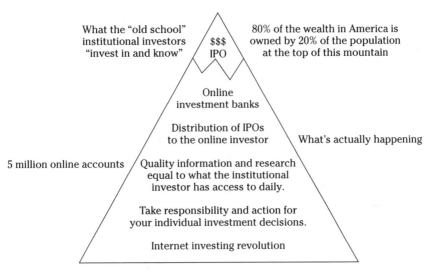

Source: IPOguys, with assistance from Pat Zito.

Matt Olejarczyk's Demystification of the IPO

I was one of the millions of people in this country who had been preconditioned to believe that IPOs were never going to be a part of my investing portfolio. The following events led to my demystification of the IPO.

When Matt Zito first approached me with the opportunity to buy IPOs online, he simply told me that he had come across a good investing opportunity he thought I might be interested in and asked me if I knew anything about investing in IPOs. The mention of IPOs made me curious, and I remembered that I had learned a little about them back in my college finance class.

Because I had known Matt for so many years and was familiar with his track record as an entrepreneur, businessperson, and shrewd investor, I realized I needed to look into his suggestion. So I pulled out the flashlight and headed to the upstairs closet to find the cardboard box that contained my old college books and files. As I started leafing through the different books and notepads, I thought more about my college days and tried to remember my finance classes. One class in particular was held early in the morning in the crescent-shaped auditorium that had a capacity of about 250 people. I had trouble recalling what my professor looked like, but his lectures were memorable, partly because money and finance weighed heavy on my mind, as I'm sure it did the other 250 college students in the class who had school loans and debt up to their ears. We all hoped that we could learn something in this class that would rescue us from years of debt.

The other reason the lectures were so memorable, though, was the professor's passion and dynamic speaking ability. He was the farthest thing from what I had anticipated a finance professor would be, considering what I had known about money and finance at that point in my life anyway. I had always figured finance, banking, and accounting were all pretty much the same thing and involved way too much manual number crunching for my liking. But our professor shined a new light on finance and captured the attention of all 250 students in that room. His lectures constantly filled the auditorium, class after class.

I was beginning to remember the lecture where we were sailing through the "typical annual performances" of the different investing vehicles, such as CDs, bonds, and stocks, and discussing the dramatic impact of compounding interest on investments over the long term. Then out of the blue, our professor dropped what the IPOguys refer to as the IPO bomb, and then dismissed class, all in one breath. The IPO bomb falls when investors first hear about the incredible profit potential of IPOs and then learn at the same time that individual investors have no access to them. We call it a bomb because that's how devastating it is to learn that this incredible investment opportunity is supposedly reserved for institutional investors and the wealthy. Here's how the professor dropped the IPO bomb on the class that day. He transitioned from something like "stocks make on average a return of 14 percent per year . . . IPOs, on the other hand, make on average return of 14 percent in one day, on the first day of trading . . . but before you get too excited, realize that IPOs are only reserved for institutional investors, not individuals like you and me. Class dismissed."

"Ouch!" is all I really remember thinking. As everyone scuttled out of the room to get to their next class, I remember sitting there, shocked and upset. I remember thinking about it, and how wrong it was that such investment vehicles existed out there, while the general public (common investors like myself) did not have access to them. How wrong that seemed, especially here in the United States, where we say, "All men are created equal." Well, I wasn't disturbed enough to start a revolution or anything. I had college things to do. I was disturbed enough, however, that I took a moment before leaving class to fold over the top corner of the page in my notebook, marking it, so that I could follow up on this disturbing concept sometime later.

As I watched myself fold over the corner of the page in my little brown notebook, there it appeared in my hands, straight out of the cardboard box I had been browsing through in my upstairs storage closet. Strangely enough, I opened it right to the IPO section of the notebook where I had folded over that page years before. When I folded that page over, little did I know that many years would go by before I would think again about IPOs and that my colleague and friend, Matt Zito, would introduce me to this revolutionary and successful investing strategy that was completely contrary to traditional academic philosophy. It's not that what the universities had taught was wrong. At the time that was a correct analysis. Times had changed, though, and the Internet was shaking things up.

With further investigation, I solidified the fact that this news was "huge." Gaining access to IPOs was an incredible new investing opportunity, and I started paper trading almost immediately. Within a few months of tracking and paper trading IPOs, I was ready to use my newly acquired knowledge and make profitable use of my money. I was ready to claim my piece of brick from the traditional financial walls that were soon to be crumbling down.

Purchasing IPOs

Now that you know you may have access to buy IPOs at the offering price, your first question has got to be, "Where can I get me some?" If you are looking for IPO shares, the most common mistake you can make is calling your traditional broker on the phone, or meeting with him or her, to see what the broker can do for you. Although it never hurts to ask, chances are the broker may not be able to allocate you any IPO shares at all, much less allocations in IPOs that you actually want. The overwhelming demand for the golden IPOs means your chances of landing any shares through a traditional brokerage firm are still slim to none. If your traditional broker/dealer is offering you shares in an IPO, you may want to stay away, *especially* if the broker called and solicited you. IPOs that are obtainable through traditional brokers are most likely going to be shares that the average investor does not want to own. Unless you are an institutional investor, there is a high likelihood that IPO shares that you get through your traditional brokerage firms are going to be losers. Any IPO worth having you are going to have to fight for, and you will not obtain it via the traditional methods.

Don't waste your time trying to obtain shares in IPOs from the traditional brokerage firms. I can almost assure you that you will be disappointed. Even if you try to obtain shares through the traditional brokerage firms, you may be limited in scope to the deals that the traditional brokerage firms are involved in. Don't be discouraged if your broker can't get you any decent IPO shares; it is a matter of simple supply and demand. We have personal relations with people who are clients of traditional brokerage firms and who have million-dollar accounts at their traditional brokerage firm but who weren't able to buy IPOs that we have been successful at buying. Pretty soon, you might just be one of those investors who is successfully buying IPOs that no one else can get at the offering price.

Once you are comfortable that the place to go for shares of worthy IPOs may not be your traditional investment broker, then you are ready to start dealing with online investment banks that are poised and ready to sell you shares of some of the hottest IPOs available. In Chapter 7, we highlight the online investment banks that offer IPOs to their clients at the offering price. Online brokers tend to offer the online individual investor a greater number of shares, and a larger assortment of deals. We anticipate that, in the future, traditional brokerage firms will start affording the individual investor an increasing portion of the total IPO pie.

Actually, those wheels are already well in motion. Mergers, acquisitions, and new business agreements are being forged at a rapid pace between the new online investment banks, venture capitalists, and the traditional brokerage firms. Regardless of the mergers and acquisitions and relationships forged, the new emerging entities will greatly benefit the individual investor. The benefits will go far beyond increased access to IPOs, and will provide the individual investor with more complete financial services.

Summary

- IPOs are the new investment vehicle available to the online individual investor.
- The process of raising capital for a company desiring to go public has remained virtually the same since the industrial revolution. The Internet is dramatically changing this.
- Online investment banks and the online individual investor are the two new key players in the capital formation process, and the two main parties likely to benefit from changes taking place in the financial and investing communities.

chapter 3

ipo performance

The mission and goal of this book is to provide you with the knowledge and tools to succeed in the world of online IPO investing. We are confident that you can make money if you follow the steps and strategies outlined in this book. We have taught people with varying levels of knowledge and experience, from high school grads to PhDs. When applying the laws of the market and successful IPO investing, previous education is not as critical as learning to recognize the information and knowledge that really matter.

The first step in preparing to invest in IPOs is to arm yourself with the knowledge of past IPO performance. Understanding IPO performance will help you make wise and responsible decisions with your IPO investments. In this chapter, we are going to take a closer look at IPO performance over both the short term and the long term. We first compare the concepts and definitions of day trading and investing. Next we look at how the IPO is similar to, yet different from, traditional investments. We then look at IPO performance over varying time periods after the IPO has started trading in the secondary market.

Trading or Investing?

Do you consider yourself a trader or an investor? The modern financial community has used the terms trading and investing so loosely over recent years that the current definitions misrepresent their true meanings. Traditional financial professionals suggest that investing is placing your money into equities over the long term. Webster's Dictionary[1] however, states that *invest* means to "put (money) to profitable use." Nowhere does the definition say anything about putting your money to profitable use over a specified time period, nor does it qualify an investment as being short or long term. In this definition, the length of time does not impact whether something is an investment or not. The act of putting your money toward a profitable future is the act of investing, over the short term as well as over the long term.

Day Trading

Right now you may be saying, "details, details, details," but it is important that you understand this detail because there is a difference. The notion that investors are investing only when holding stocks for the long term is an inaccurate connotation imposed by traditional finance professionals and academia. They may suggest that you are not investing if you are making trades over the short term. Instead, they may tag you as a day trader, which is a new term used loosely to describe a person who takes a position in a trade then exits all in the same day.

The term *day trading* has been misused by the media and has acquired a negative image as a result. Further, the business of day trading has slowly taken profits away from the traders, financial planners, and brokers on Wall Street. Traditional brokerage firms are losing clients, or at least losing portions of their clients' account balances, to individual accounts at online investment banks, which are fast accumulating huge amounts of capital at the expense of these brokerages. As a result, a battle is being waged between the new online banks and the traditional firms. This leads to plenty of mudslinging in the press, most of which is negative press about day trading. Think about it; when was the last time you heard something positive about day trading? Some traditional financial professionals also suggest that people who trade online are just gambling. They fail to give credit to or recognize any level of intelligence among educated and empowered online individual investors. This will change.

The IPOguys take a different view on day trading. The definition is accurate in that trades occur during the day, since that is when the financial markets are open (with the exception of after-hours trading). The term day trading also accurately recognizes that investors are buying and selling stocks. However, a negative connotation is being imposed by traditional brokers and financial professionals that these trades are made without adequate knowledge and consideration. The implication is that good investment decisions can be made only by trained professionals. This belief is false and inaccurate. The information and research now available to the online individual investor is just as good as the information being reviewed by the professionals. Online individual investors who take their investing seriously are as prepared as anyone else including these professionals. The traditional information, once only available to a select few, is now available to almost everyone, thus giving thousands the potential to be "professionals."

You Trade or They Trade

The traditional mutual fund manager adds stocks to or subtracts them from the investment portfolio by buying and selling them as they fall in and out of favor, depending on his or her perception of how the stocks will perform in the market. The day trader adds stocks to or subtracts them from his or her personal portfolio as they fall in and out of favor, according to the trader's perception of how the stocks will perform in the market. What is the difference between the two? Answer: One of the two actually gets paid a salary to invest your money and give advice that may or may not be any more accurate than the other person is able to surmise on his or her own. Both are trading stocks based on their best perception of how specific stocks will perform in the market. Why would we refer to what the traditional mutual fund manager does as investing and refer to the personal investing as trading when they are really the same?

Which brings us back to the first question: are you a trader or investor? We suggest that by definition, you may be both. We are all investors from the standpoint that we are putting our money to profitable use. We are traders from the standpoint that we look to achieve profits by buying and selling stocks over both the short and long term. You are an educated and informed online individual investor, armed with the knowledge and tools necessary for success.

IPO Investing Strategy

Regardless of the length of time you decide to hold your investments, we refer to the overall allocation of your money among different investment vehicles as your "personal investing strategy." Investing in IPOs as part of your overall personal investment strategy is what we refer to as your "IPO investing strategy." IPO investors invest in and trade IPOs according to a unique set of rules and performance trends characteristic of, and specific to, IPOs. Which strategy you as an IPO investor choose to follow will vary based on your risk tolerance and your need for cash.

Traditional Investments versus IPO Investments

We consider "traditional investments" to be stocks, bonds, mutual funds, and certificates of deposit. These investments are now available to buy online, although most are still purchased through stockbrokers and financial planners. Most investors own stocks and mutual funds; the latter, mutual funds, were the choice of investment for most Americans in the 1990s. Let's look at IPO performance so you can develop your own personal investing and trading style, or guidelines.

IPOs Are Considered Speculative and Risky

Once IPOs start trading publicly on one of the exchanges, there seems to be extreme volatility in the first few days of trading. Generally, there are large amounts of buying and selling in the first few days, which causes the IPO to swing both up and down in short periods of time. The volatility in one direction or another in short periods of time initially adds to the speculativeness of the investment. The current investment community classifies IPOs as "speculative investments." That means there is a high degree of risk in purchasing IPOs.

To better understand the type of risk involved in IPO investing, let's take another look at the risk versus return model by investment type. However, this time, let's add IPOs to the matrix. Table 3.1 compares IPOs "the new investment vehicle" with the traditional investments.

Investors can see that IPO investments are riskier than your average "traditional investment." The downside is that you can lose it all. The upside is that you can multiply your investments exponentially. If you invest wisely in IPOs, you may virtually eliminate the downside part of the equation and maximize the upside. First and foremost, you eliminate risk by owning shares prior to the IPO publicly trading. Second, you eliminate risk by being selective, since not all IPOs are equally attractive and lucrative. Later in the book, we discuss techniques and research tools investors can use to help in the decision-making process.

Fad Investing or Long-Term Potential?

Currently, the IPO market for Internet and technology-related IPOs is extremely hot. Before writing a book completely dedicated to IPO

Table 3.1 Long-Term Risk versus Return

Investment Type	Expected Long-Term Performance (%)		
	Low	Average	High
Low-risk (bonds/CDs)	3	5	7
Medium-risk (stock funds)	2	10	18
High-risk (single stocks)	−10	14	32
IPOs	−100	50	2000

investing, we wanted to confirm that an IPO investing strategy is a smart strategy to follow with a portion of your investments not only now, but also into the future.

Our statistical analysis of over 20 years of data has assured us that this is not a fad investing opportunity. Even though the IPO market goes through hot and cold cycles, similar to hot and cold cycles in the stock market, investing in IPOs in the primary market (buying shares at the offering price) is a solid, short-term investing strategy.

Over the past 22 years or more, IPOs on average have experienced an initial (first day) trading day gain of 15 to 20 percent. Using data provided by Jay Ritter, Professor of Finance at the University of Florida, we calculated the average first-day IPO performance since 1977 to be 17.4 percent. Table 3.2 summarizes the data, showing the number of offerings by year, and the average initial return from the offering price to the end of the first day bid or transaction price, without adjusting for market movements.

This 15 to 20 percent average gain may not be the gains of 100 to 400 or more percent that many are used to seeing with Internet IPOs, but 15 percent in a single day is certainly far above what anyone would consider an "average" return. Usually 15 to 20 percent is the kind of return you might be accustomed to looking for over the course of a year. So, although the IPO market goes through cycles, significant profits can be realized by purchasing and selling IPOs in the short term.

Why is it that IPOs have historically increased from 15 to 20 percent from the original offering price on the first day of trading? The traditional reasoning and our belief behind this first-day increase is that the underwriter is discounting the forecasted market value of the new issue to provide an incentive for investors to buy the new issue at the offering price. Investing in these typically young companies with very little operating history entails a risk that arguably justifies this discount. Knowing that these shares may be discounted and may be sold for profit in the short term, as early as the very next day, motivates most investors to own the stock at the issue price.

The end result is that everybody wins. The company launching the IPO wins because they raise the capital that they so desperately

Table 3.2 Average First-Day Initial Returns

Year	Number of Offerings	Average Initial Return (%)
77	35	18.4
78	50	25.3
79	81	22.5
80	238	49.5
81	450	16.8
82	222	15.2
83	670	23.6
84	552	11.7
85	507	13.2
86	726	10.9
87	630	10.0
88	227	9.5
89	204	13.7
90	172	13.5
91	367	17.9
92	509	12.2
93	627	15.3
94	568	13.7
95	566	20.0
96	739	17.0
97	602	13.6
98	342	28.5
99	465	68.7
Average		17.4

Source: Data courtesy of Jay Ritter, Cordell Professor of Finance at the University of Florida (http://bear.cba.ufl.edu /ritter/ipoall.htm). Used with permission.

need. The investors win because they buy into the new issue and then can turn it around for profit in a very short period of time or hold onto it for the long term. The underwriters win because they succeed in their mission of establishing the new company in the market, and they take their cut. It is beautiful, sweet, sweet music. For a detailed analogy on the traditional discounting of the initial IPO shares, see the Appendix on pages 182–186.

Largest First-Day Gainers

The hype you may see in the press about IPOs refers to a stock that doubles or more in price on the first day of trading as a "moon-shot." Prepared individual investors may have the opportunity to invest in a moonshot if they are patient and persistent. We have participated in many moonshots this year, and we can tell you from experience that they are worth the wait. What were some of the biggest IPO moonshots of all time? Table 3.3 is a listing of the top first-day gainers of all time. Companies qualified for this analysis if they were priced over $5.00 a share, with proceeds over $5,000,000, that doubled in price on the first day of trading from 1975 to 1999. All the companies were U.S. based.

Although IPOs may provide investors with the best opportunity to maximize return in the shortest period of time, investing in IPOs for the long term is a much riskier proposition. Since many young companies have little track record and operating history, there is always the chance that the company will go out of business. Ivo Welch, Professor of Finance at the Anderson Graduate School of

Table 3.3   Top 10 First-Day Gainers

	Ticker Symbol	Company	Offer Date	Offer Price	1st-Day Close	Change (%)
1	LNUX	VA Linux	12/09/99	$30	$239.25	697.5
2	TGLO	Theglobe.com	11/12/98	9	63.50	605.6
3	FDRY	Foundry Networks	11/28/99	25	156.25	525.0
4	FMKT	FreeMarkets	12/10/99	48	280.00	483.3
5	COBT	Cobalt Networks	11/05/99	22	128.00	481.8
6	MKTW	MarketWatch.com	01/15/99	17	97.50	473.5
7	AKAM	Akamai Technologies	10/29/99	26	145.19	458.4
8	CFLO	CacheFlow Systems	11/19/99	24	126.38	426.6
9	SCMR	Sycamore Networks	10/22/99	38	184.75	386.2
10	ASKJ	Ask Jeeves	07/01/99	14	64.94	363.8

Source: Supplemental data provided by ipoguys.com.

Table 3.4   Percent of Companies Dropped from Exchange or Liquidated within 5 Years

Year	Percent
80	7.0
81	29.0
82	47.0
83	13.0
84	14.0
85	22.0
86	21.0
87	18.0
88	14.0
89	11.0
90	11.0
91	8.0
92	11.0
93	10.0
Average	16.9

Source: Data courtesy of Professor Ivo Welch, Anderson Graduate School of Management at UCLA (http://www.iporesources.org).

Management at UCLA, has put together some information that highlights this fact. Table 3.4 shows failed IPOs, or the percentage of companies dropped from exchange or liquidated within 5 years of going public.

The study by Ivo Welch provides insight into long-term performance for the IPO over the long term. Tables 3.5 and 3.6 provide a historical perspective on the long-term performance of the IPO, which over the long term is not as attractive as the short-term performance. There is room to profit investing in IPOs for the savvy IPO

Table 3.5   Percent of Companies That
             Outperform the Market over
             5 Years

Year	Percent
80	40.0
81	38.0
82	18.0
83	38.0
84	42.0
85	19.0
86	29.0
87	35.0
88	28.0
89	32.0
90	30.0
91	35.0
92	31.0
93	29.0
94	28.0
95	31.0
96	32.0
97	36.0
Average	31.7

Source: Data courtesy of Professor Ivo Welch, Anderson Graduate School of Management at UCLA (http://www.iporesources.org).

investor. Table 3.5 lists the percentage of companies outperforming the market over a 5-year period immediately following their IPO. Table 3.6 shows the average return on a 5-year buy-and-hold strategy for IPOs.

Although investing in IPOs can be a high-risk proposition, several techniques can minimize risk, and in the short term, IPOs can be the single most attractive investing vehicles that exist. The volatility that surrounds most Internet and technology IPOs means profit for the prepared IPO investor.

Table 3.6   **Average Buy-and-Hold 5-Year Return**

Year	Average Raw Return (%)
80	59.0
81	38.0
82	123.0
83	78.0
84	90.0
85	12.0
86	37.0
87	35.0
88	74.0
89	74.0
90	66.0
91	93.0
92	92.0
93	67.0
94	69.0
95	42.0
96	11.0
97	7.0
Average	50.0

Source: Data courtesy of Professor Ivo Welch, Anderson Graduate School of Management at UCLA (http://www.iporesources.org).

The Future of IPO Investing

Although historical facts and figures are a factual measurement instrument that can help you become familiar with IPOs and other forms of investing, don't be blinded by the past! The dramatic effect the Internet is having on the investing community may completely alter established and commercially accepted assumptions. The rapid rate of change in business may render previous results useless. Gauges to predict future business success based on historical data analysis may become much less accurate than new models being developed that emphasize the current position in the market, strategic partnership alliances, and future business plans. Many new experts will emerge in the financial world who have never been employed by a traditional brokerage firm or even formally educated in finance. And many traditional professionals may have their talents redeployed into other roles and responsibilities.

The best way to summarize the impact that the information revolution will have on the investing community is that "the only thing constant will be change." Although this aphorism might be overplayed, it is certainly true. As the traditional walls of finance and investing come crumbling down, just like the Berlin Wall, individual investors need to learn how to profit from new opportunities created by the free flow of information over the Internet. IPOs may provide the best opportunity. Over the next couple of years, however, new preferred strategies to achieving profits will emerge. Be conscious of the past, but keep an open mind. Invest in companies that hold great future promise and that embrace new technology and especially change. Regardless of your success, never overleverage yourself so that you are dependent on any one investing strategy. Try to maintain an investment strategy that includes diversification.

That's that!

We hope we have dispelled any misconceptions surrounding the IPO. Further, we hope you understand why the general public's confusion about IPOs can mean profit for you. Most importantly, we hope you have learned enough to be anxious to take action.

In Chapter 4, we examine today's hottest IPOs—Internet IPOs.

Summary

- Initial public offerings provide one of the best and newest investing opportunities for the individual investor.
- You may achieve the highest returns in IPO investing by purchasing IPOs in the primary market at the offering price (prior to the secondary market when they are actively trading on the open market).
- Historical data shows us that large profits can be made by investing in IPOs and can be achieved over the short term.

Sometimes large profits may be achieved on the first day of trading. Investing in IPOs for the long term can be equally lucrative, although there is a much higher level of risk involved in holding the shares for the long term.

- Historical analysis may become less indicative of future performance in financial markets. Be cognizant of new opportunities and valuation methodologies.

chapter 4

internet ipos

Whether you are an experienced investor or brand-new to the world of investing, if you are looking to make incredible returns with your money . . . remember these two words, "Internet IPO."

You may have seen articles or news headlines about Internet IPOs that double or triple in price on the first day of trading. The realization that the Internet will have a dramatic impact on our lives is causing technology and Internet stock prices to go through the roof. Why are Internet IPOs so hot right now? The driving force behind Internet IPOs is the belief that the Internet will fundamentally change the face of American business and affect virtually every facet of our society.

The explosion of the Internet economy and online trading has helped support the longest bull market in the history of our country. E-commerce transactions (consumer direct purchases over the Internet) are just beginning to gain momentum, which may continue to drive Internet stocks to further heights.

When will this tremendous momentum end? No one knows for sure. However, all indicators point toward continued expansion in the technology and Internet sectors into the foreseeable future. The explosive growth of the Internet is yet to be fully realized, and Internet IPOs stand at the heart of all this development.

Internet Stocks—A Different Investing Strategy

Investing in Internet IPOs requires a slightly different investing strategy than normal. The profit-conscious investor who likes to study company financial data before making stock purchases will find the Internet stock craze mind-baffling. Start-up technology and Internet companies with losses in the millions of dollars and terrible financial data launch incredibly successful IPOs. They raise millions of dollars, or in some cases, close to a billion dollars of working capital through the sale of their IPO shares when the company becomes public.

Some of these companies have never turned a profit, nor do they foresee making a profit in the near future. Yet these shares are the hottest things since the advent of television. A revolution is taking place.

Why are the stocks of companies that are currently losing money being so eagerly accepted by investors in the market? Why are the Internet and technology companies valued at such abnormally high levels? The valuations are based on future earnings potential and the belief that the efficiencies gained through the Internet will lead to tremendous future profits. As with any high-growth industry, there will undoubtedly be many mergers and acquisitions, which could delay the realization of profits. Some companies that survive the Internet shakeout over the coming years will emerge as enormously profitable Titans. Microsoft is a notable example of a company that has been able to capitalize on the Internet and technology movement, and plenty of other companies will succeed as well. Investments today in one of these titanic companies of tomorrow may yield excellent dividends in the future. The strength of your belief that specific Internet companies will generate projected future revenues and profits tends to be directly proportional to your level of investment in the Internet and technology sectors for both the long and short term.

Now that you have learned about both the short-term and long-term performance of the IPO from the statistics presented in

Figure 4.1   Average First-Day IPO Performance

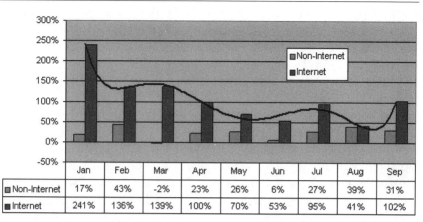

	Jan	Feb	Mar	Apr	May	Jun	Jul	Aug	Sep
Non-Internet	17%	43%	-2%	23%	26%	6%	27%	39%	31%
Internet	241%	136%	139%	100%	70%	53%	95%	41%	102%

Source: Data from Ostman's Alert-IPO (www.alert-ipo.com). Used with permission.

Chapter 3, let's take a look specifically at the Internet IPO performance, as shown in Figure 4.1.

Not convinced that this is the greatest investing opportunity of the century? Table 4.1 reveals how the IPO market has heated up during the past two years. The table shows return on investment if you were to buy and hold every IPO between January 1, 1998, through December 1, 1999. We calculated the average return using intraday market prices on Monday, December 6, 1999.

Table 4.1   Two-Year Buy and Hold Return

Year	Number of Offerings	Change from Offering Price (%)
98	365	49.2
99	505	147.6
Total	870	106.3

Source: Ostman's Alert-IPO (www.ostman.com/alert-ipo) provided the list of IPOs to calculate these returns. Used with permission.

It is difficult to ignore the statistics in Table 4.1, especially if you have been preconditioned by any financial experts who might suggest that the returns per the classic risk versus return chart are what you should expect. The Internet IPO may be one of the best, if not the absolute best investment opportunity currently available to the individual investor. There has never been a better time to invest at least a small portion of your money into the technology and Internet sector.

Time to Get to the "Good Stuff"

Up to this point, we have covered mostly the basics to provide a sturdy framework for IPO investors. From this point forward, our information will benefit IPO investors at every level of expertise. If you are a beginner and IPO investing is such a new concept that it reads about as easily as Egyptian hieroglyphics, do not fear. Memorizing all the details and definitions is not important right now. You can always come back and use this book as a reference. The IPO Glossary at the end of the book is especially good for referencing terms at a later date. If you have a basic understanding of the material covered up to this point, that is all that matters.

In Chapter 5, we review a few basic investing strategies and get into specific Web sites devoted to helping the IPO investor. We also discuss the single most important document used by the IPO investor in evaluating IPOs, the prospectus.

Summary

- The technology and Internet-related sectors are currently realizing rapid growth and expansion. Investing in technology and Internet IPOs provides the best new opportunity for high returns on your investment.

- Including IPO investing as part of your overall investment strategy has good long-term profit potential. As the investing community focus shifts away from technology and Internet-related companies, other sectors will come into favor and provide the IPO investor continued opportunities to achieve higher than average returns on their investment.

chapter 5

preinvesting preparation and research

strategies, evaluation of ipos, web sites

The aim of this book is to teach you how to make money investing in IPOs, to help organize and simplify your research, and to minimize the time it takes for you to make good IPO investing decisions. This chapter deals with the organization and simplification of research, and general preparations that you need to make prior to investing in IPOs.

Prior to Investing

There are two main investing strategies that every investor can follow, regardless of the investments they will be making. The first is known as diversification, and the second is referred to as "paper trading."

Diversification
You have heard the cliché, "Don't put all your eggs in one basket." The same holds true for your investment portfolio. Spreading out your investment risk over multiple investments is what as known as

diversification. Diversification should be a very important strategy for every investment portfolio.

If you do not have the time or knowledge to diversify your investments on your own, find a broker you trust who can diversify your investment pie. How much of the pie you let the broker manage is up to you. The amount of money you have available to invest obviously plays a role in your allocation decision. Table 5.1 is a client study illustrating the evaluation of investment strategies.

"Paper Trade" First

Another highly recommended strategy before doing any individual investing, IPO investing or other, is to "paper trade." Paper trading means setting up a make-believe account with a set amount of pretend money, then buying and selling stocks, IPOs, and so on "on paper" using the money in your pretend account. This way, you can learn from your mistakes without throwing away your good hard-earned money because of inexperience. Paper trading will also help you build confidence before you make your first trade.

Personal Considerations

Money

The first and most basic decision you need to make as you begin investing in IPOs is how much money to invest in volatile stocks. How much you set aside for IPOs is up to you, but we advise against taking all your savings and wildly throwing it into your self-managed online account. It is better to allocate a portion of your money into your online account, especially until you are comfortable with your investment decisions. How much money you have in your total investing portfolio is the largest factor in determining how much you set aside for this aggressive investing strategy. How much is enough? The amount may be a portion of your savings that you are comfortable watching expand and contract like a pair of lungs. Remember that investing in IPOs is an aggressive growth strategy often characterized by volatility. There is a high likelihood that the IPO you invest in will move significantly from the price you bought it at, one way or the other.

Table 5.1 Client Study: Ozarks Limited

Name:	Ozarks Limited
Location:	Camdenton, MO
Online Accounts:	Wit Capital, E*TRADE

Length of time trading IPOs online: 8 months

Amount invested in IPO portfolio (% of total investing portfolio): 2%

Profits/(Losses):	$32,250.00/($2,130)

IPOs, # shares, status:			
	Miningco	BarnesandNoble	US Search
	Onemain	Wit Capital	Allscripts
	Prodigy	BackwebTech	Medscape
	Healtheon	DR. Koop	Shopnow
	Boyd's	Stamps	DataReturn
	Multex	Autobytel	CAIS
	NetObjects		

Best Trade:	Healtheon, 200 shares, profit=$12,100.00
Worst Trade:	Boyds Bearstone bears, 100 shares, loss=$620
Favorite IPO Web Sites:	Yahoo, Hoover's
Most Useful Strategies:	Before 10/01/99: Forget about research and buy every new Internet IPO offered. After 10/01/99: Buy every new Internet stock focused on communications, international Internet providers, investment firms, e-commerce in the areas of services (mortgages online, shopping, insurance online, etc.) and companies manufacturing Internet backbone technologies such as routers.
Pitfalls to Avoid:	Buying IPOs which price at the low end or below their predicted price.
Other:	Now, with online trading, it is very common to have 1,000s of small share trades per day whereas before, trade quantities were in larger blocks. With the small trades, the price of a stock fluctuates much more than before. The small trader can profit from this phenomenon. In other words, 5,000 traded shares of a company with 65,000,000 shares outstanding can affect the stock price immensely when the 5,000 shares are traded in 100 share blocks, one after another. (50 separate trades at $\frac{1}{16}$ a share difference between bid and ask can drop or raise the stock as much as 1.00 to 3.00.

Investing and Trading Tendencies

Everyone has his or her own personal investing style. Some people are motivated by fear, others by opportunity; and some people are just not motivated at all. If you are reading this book, then chances are you are not the latter, but are ready to begin taking control of your financial future by capitalizing on IPO investing strategies. Before you begin, you need to identify the kind of personal investing and trading tendencies you have as a part of who you are. Table 5.2 is a client study showing an awareness of personal limits.

Although we all think we know ourselves pretty well, our actions can surprise even ourselves when money is on the line. Learning how you may act in certain situations prior to actually making decisions will greatly benefit you under any investing or trading strategy. Answering the following questions will reveal

---

Table 5.2   Client Study: The Jergensens

Name:	The Jergensens
Location:	Baltimore, MD
Online Accounts:	Wit Capital

Length of time trading IPOs online:	3 months

Amount invested in IPO portfolio (% of total investing portfolio):	$2,000

Profits/(Losses):	$800.00/($0)

IPOs, # shares, status:	WWF Entertainment, 100, Sold

Favorite IPO Web Sites:	Redherring

Most Useful Strategies:	To have access to a computer early in the day so you can move quickly on any changes. Most likely we would get in and then sell quickly to make a profit. Always research before getting involved. We learned to use the Internet to check on our stocks often to notice any changes.

Pitfalls to Avoid:	Always have a clear understanding of what your limits are, how much you are willing to risk, and what the process involves.

basic personal characteristics that can influence your IPO trading strategy: How strong is your "gut" at withstanding volatility? (We call it the "iron gut" factor.) How anxious are you to trade or invest in IPOs?

Dealing with Volatility   Withstanding market volatility is a major consideration for the individual investor prior to entering the IPO market. By nature, IPOs are extremely volatile over the short term. Some people simply cannot handle watching such large price swings from day to day. If you are one of these people, don't worry. There are ways to get around daily price watching. You can set "limit orders" on your positions or holdings to automatically buy or sell when the securities reach a specified price target. Some online investment banks allow you to set up alarms on your account that notify you via e-mail or pager when the stock reaches a specified price. That way, your investments aren't automatically bought or sold; you are just immediately notified and can make a decision from there. You will fully understand how well you deal with market volatility only after you have been through both the highs and lows in the market. You may not truly know the strength of your gut until the money is on the line. The only way to prepare yourself and to develop an iron gut is by paper trading, a strategy discussed earlier.

The best way to strengthen your gut and ease any stress that you experience when beginning your IPO investing journey is to make a profitable first trade. This is key to getting IPO investors off to a good start. Making a profit on your first trade, and then reinvesting the profits in the markets will soothe even the weakest gut. Individual investors who make enough profit from their first trade (or couple of trades) can pull out their initial investment and only reinvest their profits.

Making a Good First Trade   To help ensure a successful first trade, do your homework and be selective. The most critical thing to learn from this chapter is *be selective.* Only invest in IPOs that you are absolutely 100 percent certain will be successful in the open market, especially for your first trade. In the client studies we performed in preparation for this book, this was one of the main points most common among our respondents. We enjoyed the clear, concise advice from "Bill and Kyla" (see Table 5.3) who suggest, "Don't jump at just any IPO, wait for the "HOT" ones!"

We also thoroughly enjoyed the feedback we received from "LesTaxes" (see Table 5.4) who agrees that being selective is a major key to your early IPO investing success. (We found the name "LesTaxes" ironic and hilarious considering the profits this client achieved in just 11 months).

After paper trading IPOs for a while, it becomes easier to identify which IPOs are hot and which are not. Exactly how long it takes to gain confidence in your ability to identify winning IPOs will vary by investor and depend on the number of IPOs you successfully paper trade.

Dealing with Anxiety Being selective and waiting for a golden IPO may seem obvious. However, many investors are so anxious to get into their first IPO that they overlook this major detail and end up buying any IPO they can get their hands on. This brings us to our

Table 5.3 Client Study: Bill and Kyla

Name:	Bill and Kyla		
Location:	Bear, DE		
Online Accounts:	Wit Capital		
Length of time trading IPOs online:			3 months
Amount invested in IPO portfolio (% of total investing portfolio):			15%
Profits/(Losses):	$800.00/($0)		
IPOs, # shares, status:	Company	Shares	Status
	Splitrock Services	100	Sold
	Medscape	100	Still Own
	Charter	100	Still Own
Favorite IPO Web Sites:	Redherring, Ostman, Smart Money Interactive		
Most Useful Strategies:	Know the pricing date of the IPO so you ave a better chance of being ready for and getting them.		
Pitfalls to Avoid:	Don't jump at just any IPO, wait for the "HOT" ones!		

Table 5.4   Client Study: LesTaxes

Name:	LesTaxes
Location:	Erie, PA
Online Accounts:	Wit Capital, E*TRADE, FBR.com

Length of time trading IPOs online: 11 months

Amount invested in IPO portfolio (% of total investing portfolio):	"As much as possible. I borrowed a few thousand from my savings to get started initially, but have paid back the principal. I am rolling profits back and opening new online accounts to increase my chances of getting IPOs."
Profits/(Losses):	$35,000.00/($1,000)

IPOs, # shares, status:			
	OneMain	Miningco	Webstakes
	Prodigy	Wit Capital	Mpath
	Healtheon	BackwebTech	AppliedTheory
	Calico	DR. Koop	NetPerceptions
	BarnesandNoble	Stamps	Shopnow
	Mail	Autobytel	CAIS
	Multex	US Search	NetObjects
	SplitRock	TriZetto	The Knot
	VerticalNet	Charter	

Best Trade:	Healtheon, buy 100 shares @ $8, sell 100 shares @ $54, profit = $4,600
Worst Trade:	NetObjects, buy 100 shares @ $12, sell 100 shares @ $7 loss = $500
Favorite IPO Web Sites:	Redherring, Gaskins, Multex, IPO.com
Most Useful Strategies:	Research as much as possible. Stay on top of trends/hot issues.
Pitfalls to Avoid:	Don't buy every IPO that is out there.
Other:	Don't be discouraged if you make a mistake . . . simply learn from it. Be happy with any profit you decide to take, even if you sell "too early" and the stock continues to go higher.

second personal investing and trading tendency, how anxious you are to trade. This is the last but not least of personal considerations when entering the IPO investing arena. Once you see the potential profits you can achieve by investing in IPOs, you will be unsettled to say the least, no matter how level-headed you might consider yourself. The volatility and potential profitability of IPO investing can unsettle virtually anyone. When you find yourself becoming anxious to get in there and make a trade, above all else, be patient and wait it out. IPOs worth investing in can be difficult to come by, and are worth waiting for. Share allocations at the offering price are becoming increasingly available for the individual investor, so just because you are anxious to trade, don't settle for an IPO that you are not 100 percent excited about.

Avoid Buying Shares on the First Day of Trading

The most common mistake inexperienced IPO investors make is to buy shares on the first day of trading when they are not allocated shares at the offering price. This is generally the last thing you should want to do, especially if it is a highly anticipated IPO. Even though this may be the IPO you really wanted, don't buy it at the inflated price that normally surrounds a red-hot IPO on the first day of trading. IPO performance on the first couple days of trading is extremely volatile and unpredictable. Further, there is usually so much volume on the first day that your trade may not execute for an undetermined period of time. This may be especially true of limit orders, which take second priority, and do not trade until all market orders have been executed. Even market orders placed early might not execute until the price of the stock has moved 5, 10, 20, or even 50 points! Buying IPOs on the first day online can be a potentially disastrous course of action.

Table 5.5   Client Study: Silverstreak

Name:	Silverstreak
Location:	Bedford, PA
Online Accounts:	Wit Capital, E*TRADE

Length of time trading IPOs online:	11 months

Amount invested in IPO portfolio (% of total investing portfolio):	27%

Profits/(Losses):	$21,107.00/($308)

IPOs, # shares, status:

About.com	BarnesandNoble	US Search
Onemain	Wit Capital	Allscripts
Prodigy	Mpath (HearMe)	Medscape
Applied Theory	PLX Tech	Shopnow
Cobalt Networks	Stamps	DataReturn
Mail.com	Autobytel	CAIS
NetObjects	iTurf	VerticalNet
StudentAdvantage	2,900 total shares	

Best Trade:	VerticalNet, 100 shares buy @ $16/share, sell @ $140.25, profit = $12,425
Worst Trade:	BarnesandNoble, on 400 shares, net loss = $152
Favorite IPO Web Sites:	IPO.com, Gaskins, Hoover's
Most Useful Strategies:	"Gut" it out on the poor buy decisions, buy low sell high
Pitfalls to Avoid:	Don't be too greedy. Set a profit strategy and timing and stick to it.
Other:	Counsel with the IPOguys.

Other Advice from Client Studies—Preinvesting Research Is Critical

Some common opinions that rang true in many of our client studies is that research is of critical importance as well as picking a profit target and then staying with it (see Tables 5.5 and 5.6). There is no substitute to doing your homework. Many information sources are available to the IPO investor to help you make responsible IPO investing decisions, and it is important to know how to use these sources wisely.

Table 5.6 Client Study: Steve Hunter

Name:	Steve Hunter
Location:	Cleveland, OH
Online Accounts:	Wit Capital

Length of time trading IPOs online: 3 months

Amount invested in IPO portfolio (% of total investing portfolio):   2%

Profits/(Losses): $2,600.00/($0)

IPOs, # shares, status:	Company	Shares	Status
	BSquare	100	Sold
	Splitrock Services	100	Sold
	Data Return Corp.	100	Still Own
	Medscape	100	Still Own
	TriZetto Group	100	Still Own

Best Trade:	BSquare bought 100 shares @ $15.00 sold 100 shares @ $30.50 = $1,550.00 profit.
Favorite IPO Web Sites:	Red Herring, Hoover's, CNET, Reuters, SmartPortfolio.com
Most Useful Strategies:	Shoot for 100% profit minimum

Information Source 1—The Prospectus

The single most important document available to the IPO investor is the company's prospectus. Investors may want to spend a majority of their time researching this document. A prospectus is created to formally communicate important details of the offering with potential investors. The prospectus by law must be filed and sent to the Securities Exchange Commission (SEC), the governing body for all companies that go public.

When considering an investment in an IPO, you will be able to review a preliminary version of the prospectus. The preliminary

prospectus is basically the same as the prospectus; however, it is missing details such as offering price and pricing date. The preliminary prospectus is also known as the red herring.

The prospectus provides potential investors with a complete analysis of the potential risks associated with investing in the registered company and typically includes the following subjects:

Front Page

Table of Contents

Summary

Risk Factors

Use of Proceeds

Dividend Policy

Capitalization

Dilution

Financial Data

Management Discussion, Analysis of Financial Conditions, and Results of Operations

Business

Management

Certain Transactions

Principal and Selling Stockholders

Description of Capital Stock

Shares Eligible for Future Share

Underwriting

Legal Matters

Experts

Additional Information

Index to Financial Statements

The prospectus is generally written by the company's lawyers and therefore can be cumbersome and sometimes confusing. Certain subjects within the prospectus help investors evaluate a company. The following list describes the key subjects each investor should review prior to buying shares in any IPO.

1. *The Front Page.* The opener page lists basic and yet extremely important information about the offering, including (a) the company name, (b) the number of shares being offered, (c) the estimated price range, and (d) the underwriters. Figure 5.1 shows an example cover page of a prospectus. It highlights that Careerbuilder.com is selling a total of 4,500,000 shares in the initial public offering. The stock is being sold to the public for an estimated price of $10–$12 per share. The underwriters are Credit Suisse First Boston, BancBoston Robertson Stephens, Hambrecht & Quist, and Friedman Billings Ramsey.

   (a) The company name is important because a good name can launch an IPO simply because it is recognized and well respected. CBS Marketwatch.com and Perot Systems are examples of companies whose IPOs were well received by the investing community due in part to name recognition.

   (b) The number of shares being offered influences the success of an IPO. An imbalance of supply and demand will cause the IPO to rise or fall. If the number of shares being offered is greater than the demand for the IPO, the result is often a flat or poor performing IPO. In contrast, a small number of shares with a large demand will result in an imbalance favoring demand, which often creates an escalating aftermarket price, and successful IPO. Determining whether the demand meets or exceeds the supply of a particular IPO is one of the keys to IPO investing success.

   (c) The price of an IPO also affects supply and demand. Investors might not be willing to invest their money in companies with an inflated offering price, causing the IPO stock price to fall.

Figure 5.1   Careerbuilder Prospectus Cover Page

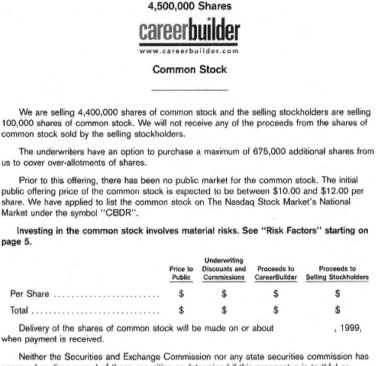

SUBJECT TO COMPLETION, DATED MAY 5, 1999

4,500,000 Shares

careerbuilder

www.careerbuilder.com

Common Stock

We are selling 4,400,000 shares of common stock and the selling stockholders are selling 100,000 shares of common stock. We will not receive any of the proceeds from the shares of common stock sold by the selling stockholders.

The underwriters have an option to purchase a maximum of 675,000 additional shares from us to cover over-allotments of shares.

Prior to this offering, there has been no public market for the common stock. The initial public offering price of the common stock is expected to be between $10.00 and $12.00 per share. We have applied to list the common stock on The Nasdaq Stock Market's National Market under the symbol "CBDR".

Investing in the common stock involves material risks. See "Risk Factors" starting on page 5.

	Price to Public	Underwriting Discounts and Commissions	Proceeds to CareerBuilder	Proceeds to Selling Stockholders
Per Share	$	$	$	$
Total	$	$	$	$

Delivery of the shares of common stock will be made on or about   , 1999, when payment is received.

Neither the Securities and Exchange Commission nor any state securities commission has approved or disapproved of these securities or determined if this prospectus is truthful or complete. Any representation to the contrary is a criminal offense.

Credit Suisse First Boston

BancBoston Robertson Stephens

Hambrecht & Quist

Friedman Billings Ramsey

Prospectus dated   , 1999.

The information in this prospectus is not complete and may be changed. We may not sell these securities until the registration statement filed with the Securities and Exchange Commission is effective. This prospectus is not an offer to sell these securities and it is not soliciting an offer to buy these securities in any state where the offer or sale is not permitted.

Source: Courtesy of Careerbuilder (www.careerbuilder.com). Used with permission.

(d) Finally, the underwriters play a huge part in determining the success of an IPO in the aftermarket. Credible underwriters will limit distribution and support the IPO regardless of demand. This may involve the underwriter buying shares of the IPO to protect the market price.

2. *Risk Factors.* These are key in determining whether to buy shares in a particular IPO. Look to see whether the company has ever defaulted on any loans, or if any lawsuits are pending against the company currently that could vastly affect the short-term value of the stock. Find out whether the managers running the company are experienced and have good track records (see item 5).

3. *Use of Proceeds.* What will the company do with the millions of dollars they raise from investors? If the company is going to use the capital for paying off large amounts of debt, this should be a major concern. When young and aggressive companies spend a majority of the capital toward building up their revenue and growing their company for the long term, they often perform well in the market. This is especially true if they have a good marketing plan.

4. *Business.* This section is critical in deciding whether to invest in IPOs. What does this company do? What is it selling? Who are its competitors? Are any of its competitors' leaders in the market? What prices and values are the competitors' stock currently trading at? Is there room in the marketplace for this young company? Can this young company become the leader in the market? These are just a few of the questions you should ask yourself when reading the section on the company's business. Understanding the business and believing that the company can achieve considerable and sustainable future profits are critical factors in selecting a successful IPO.

5. *Management.* Who is currently running the company? Has the current management had previous experience in running a successful company? Upper management with an excellent track record for high performance will definitely

have a positive impact on the perception by the investment community of the company, and therefore on the stock price.

6. *Principal and Selling Stockholders.* Is the founder of this young upstart selling a majority of his or her shares? If so, you might not want to invest in this company. Who are the existing shareholders? Are they successful venture capitalists? Many of the Internet upstarts are being funded privately by venture capitalists. Venture capitalists or angels are individuals and companies that help fund fledgling companies in the very beginning of operations. Venture capitalists provide working capital for the upstarts in exchange for large percentages of stock, generally at very low prices. When an Internet company goes public, the venture capitalists shares can be worth millions of dollars more than their original investment. Look for venture capitalists with great track records. Who invested early on with Ebay, Ubid, VerticalNet, and Healtheon? The prospectus will verify who has, or which companies have, a financial stake from the beginning in the company. We discuss this topic in more detail later in this book.

7. *Underwriting.* What company or companies are selling (or issuing) stock to investors? With the advent of the Internet, the underwriting field is totally changing the distribution system of issuing shares in IPOs. Traditionally, the major underwriters issued shares to large institutions such as mutual fund companies, universities, insurance companies, and wealthy individuals with portfolios in the millions. Table 5.7 lists some of the best known underwriters in the United States with established credibility. Individual investors should look for deals that have backing from a minimum of one of the underwriters in this list.

8. *Financial Statements.* The financial statements of the company will include their auditors' report, balance sheets, statements of operations, stockholders' equity, and cash flow statements. Investors can review revenue for the past 1 to 3 years, the company's income or loss from operations,

---
Table 5.7 Underwriter List

Goldman Sachs

Morgan Stanley Dean Witter

Credit Suisse First Boston

Merrill Lynch

Donaldson Lufkin & Jenrette

BancBoston Robertson Stephens

Bear Sterns & Co., Inc.

Lehman Brothers

JP Morgan & Co.

Hambrecht & Quist

Salomon Smith Barney

Volpe Brown Whelan & Co.

CIBC Oppenheimer

Paine Webber

BT Alexander Brown

Friedman Billings Ramsey & Co.

Thomas Weissel Partners LLC

---

and cash flow that the company currently holds. Cash flow is an important factor to consider when reading through the financials because it is difficult to "fudge," whereas other financial data can be "doctored" to make the company look healthier than it actually is. In the Internet and technology sector, however, future earnings potential is a factor that is being valued increasingly higher by investors, more so than current financials.

Information Source 2—Internet Web Sites

One of the words you will commonly come across as you start researching IPOs is "hot." How do you determine which IPOs are really hot and which are not? The key to answering that question is having quality information available to you on a consistent basis.

The Internet boasts a wealth of information about investing in IPOs. The following Web sites provide excellent information to investors. Most of the Web sites provide free research, and some of them offer a fee-based subscription.

Ostman's Alert-IPO
http://www.ostman.com

This Web site definitely needs to be at the top of your list of sites to bookmark (see Figures 5.2 and 5.3). Of all the sites we reviewed, this one provides the greatest amount of free IPO data. One of its best features is that Ostman pays particular attention to providing the most accurate and timely pricing calendar, which is absolutely critical to the IPO investor. Knowing when an IPO is going

---

Figure 5.2   Ostman's Alert-IPO Page

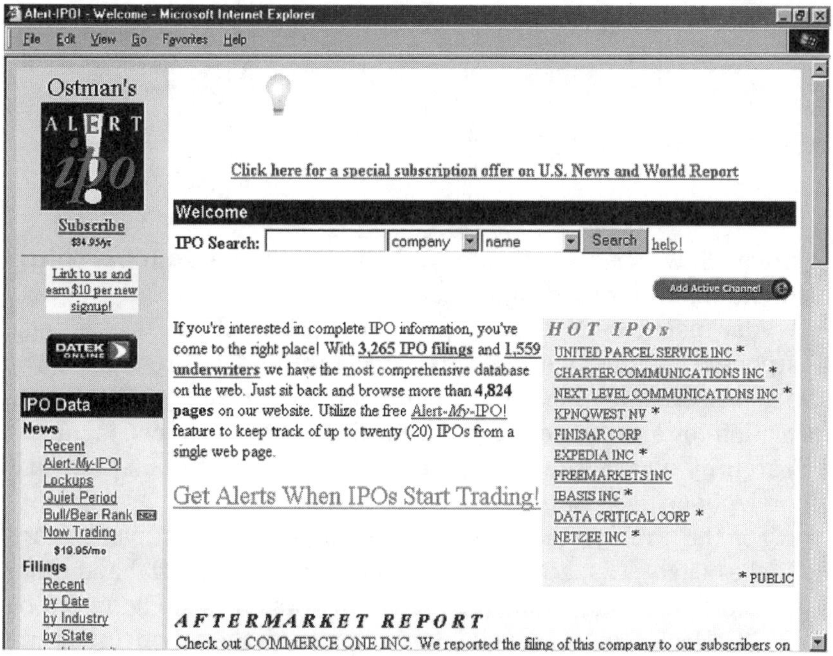

Source: Courtesy of Ostman's Alert-IPO (www.ostman.com). Used with permission.

Figure 5.3 Aftermarket Report Page

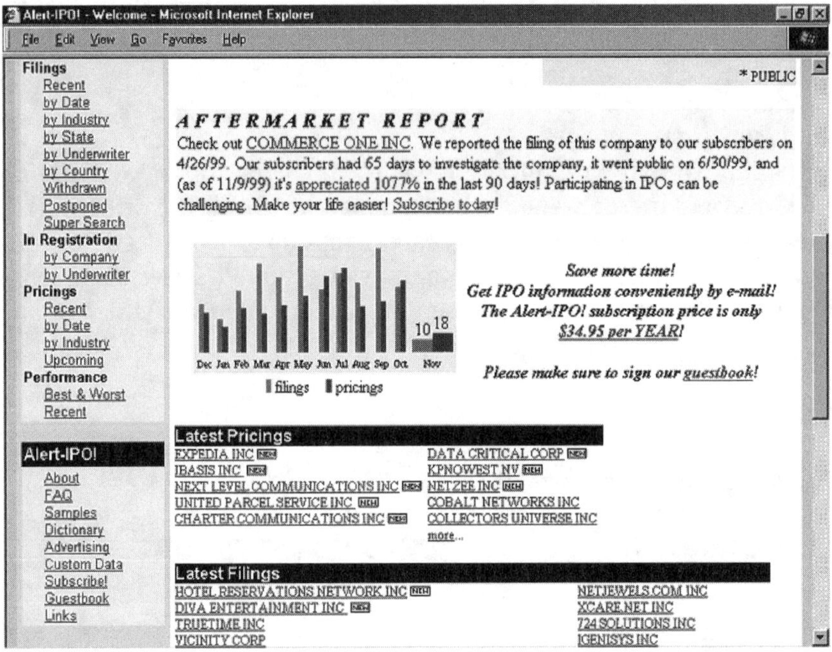

Source: Courtesy of Ostman's Alert-IPO (www.ostman.com). Used with permission.

to price allows the IPO investor to be better prepared to reconfirm a conditional offer (see Figure 5.4).

Also listed on the home page are the latest pricings, filings, postponements, and withdrawals, which are updated regularly. The site allows users to search for abbreviated company prospectus information for any upcoming or recent IPO in several ways, including a search by underwriter, company name, ticker symbol, state, city, zip, telephone, description, and shareholder.

For the abbreviated version of the prospectus, Ostman's Alert-IPO takes each prospectus and filters out the excess legal and other boilerplate language from the full-length version (see Figure 5.5 on page 72). Having only the key information from the prospectus is an

Figure 5.4 Upcoming IPOs Page

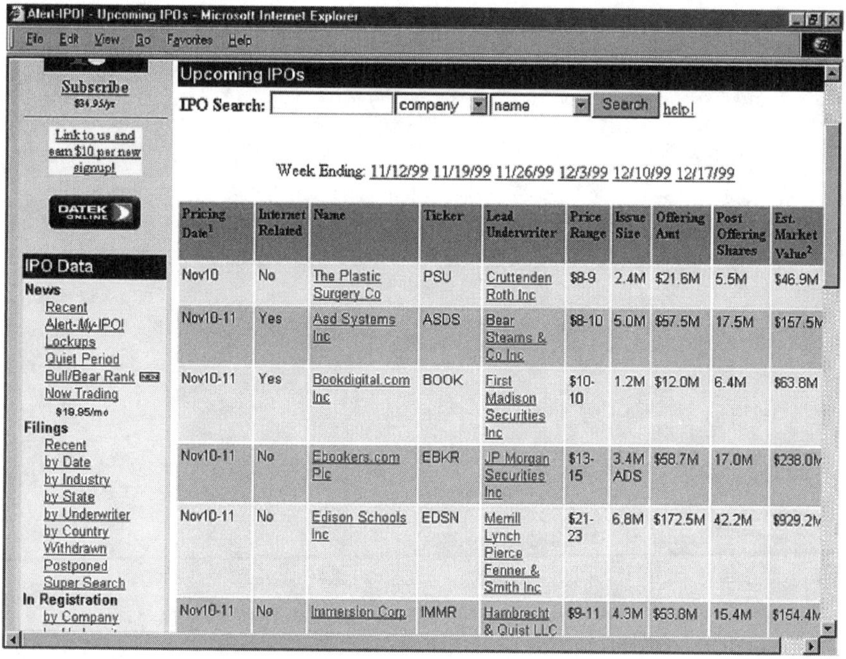

Pricing Date[1]	Internet Related	Name	Ticker	Lead Underwriter	Price Range	Issue Size	Offering Amt	Post Offering Shares	Est. Market Value[2]
Nov10	No	The Plastic Surgery Co	PSU	Cruttenden Roth Inc	$8-9	2.4M	$21.6M	5.5M	$46.9M
Nov10-11	Yes	Asd Systems Inc	ASDS	Bear Stearns & Co Inc	$8-10	5.0M	$57.5M	17.5M	$157.5M
Nov10-11	Yes	Bookdigital.com Inc	BOOK	First Madison Securities Inc	$10-10	1.2M	$12.0M	6.4M	$63.8M
Nov10-11	No	Ebookers.com Plc	EBKR	JP Morgan Securities Inc	$13-15	3.4M ADS	$58.7M	17.0M	$238.0M
Nov10-11	No	Edison Schools Inc	EDSN	Merrill Lynch Pierce Fenner & Smith Inc	$21-23	6.8M	$172.5M	42.2M	$929.2M
Nov10-11	No	Immersion Corp	IMMR	Hambrecht & Quist LLC	$9-11	4.3M	$53.8M	15.4M	$154.4M

Source: Courtesy of Ostman's Alert-IPO (www.ostman.com). Used with permission.

especially nice time saving feature. Another great service Ostman's Alert-IPO recently began providing is a section called "Bull/Bear IPO Rankings," where upcoming IPOs are ranked according to technical indicators (see Figure 5.6 on page 73).

You will also find two sections in the Web site where you can view expiring quiet periods and expiring lockup periods—two key dates for IPO investors (see Figures 5.7 on page 74 and 5.8 on page 75). (See glossary for definitions of quiet and lockup periods.)

Free sections available

Subscription (fee-based) service: Ostman's Premium (subscription) service

Figure 5.5   Charter Communications Inc. Page

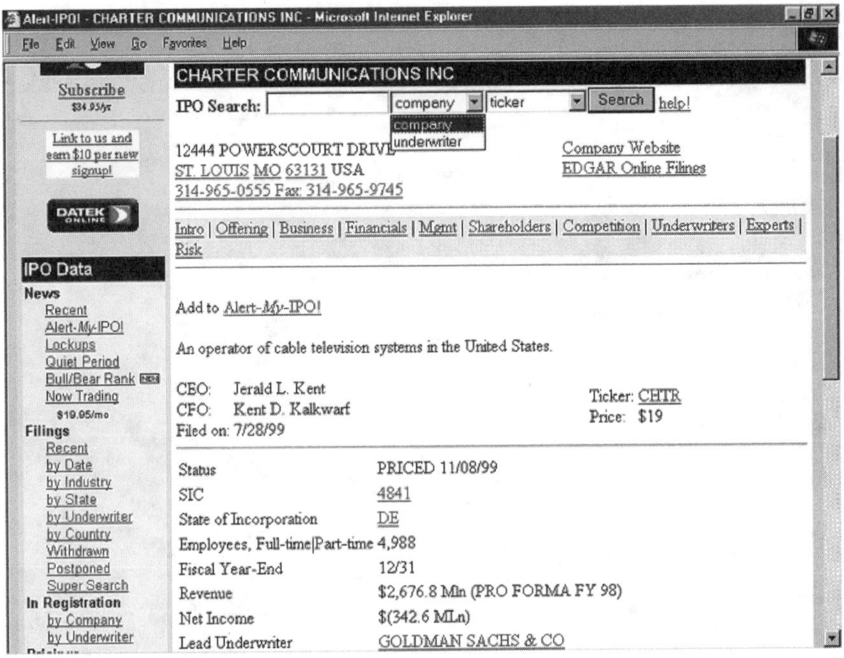

Source: Courtesy of Ostman's Alert-IPO (www.ostman.com). Used with permission.

Hoover's IPO Central
http://www.ipocentral.com
http://www.hoovers.com

IPO Central is a feature of Hoover's Online, which is one of the most informative and comprehensive business information sites on the Web. You will find many free benefits, such as the ability to receive free stock quotes (delayed) and to set up a stock portfolio (see Figure 5.9 on pages 76–77).

Be sure to register for the Hoover's IPO Update newsletter. This will allow you to receive free weekly IPO updates via e-mail, through which you can keep track of recent filings and pricings (see Figure 5.10 on page 78).

This is a great section for beginners looking to invest in IPOs. Every week, IPO Central features IPOs of special interest

Figure 5.6 Bull/Bear IPO Rankings Page

Source: Courtesy of Ostman's Alert-IPO (www.ostman.com). Used with permission.

with in-depth commentary on the featured IPO(s). The IPO Score-card provides valuable IPO performance information (see Figure 5.11 on page 79).

This was the first Web site we found that allowed us to view IPOs by underwriter, which is an extremely valuable tool for finding the IPOs your broker is handling. Knowing this information in advance allows you more time to research IPOs that you are considering purchasing. This and other more complex and in-depth search filtering capabilities are now available at several IPO Web sites in addition to Hoover's IPO Central.

We interviewed Kenan Pollack, the Money editor at Hoover's.[1]

IPOguys: What value does your Web site add to the individual IPO investor?

Figure 5.7 Quiet Period Page

Company	Ticker	Trading	Expires
IGO CORP	IGOC	10/14/99	11/8/99
NETCENTIVES INC	NCNT	10/14/99	11/8/99
NETRADIO CORP	NETR	10/14/99	11/8/99
RESOURCEPHOENIX.COM INC	RPCX	10/14/99	11/8/99
CYSIVE INC	CYSV	10/15/99	11/9/99
EPCOS AG	EPC	10/15/99	11/9/99
JACADA LTD	JCDA, JCDAV, JCDAY	10/15/99	11/9/99
QUICKLOGIC CORP	QUIK	10/15/99	11/9/99
WOMEN COM NETWORKS INC	WOMN	10/15/99	11/9/99
MARTHA STEWART LIVING OMNIMEDIA INC	MSO	10/19/99	11/13/99
PC TEL INC	PCTI	10/19/99	11/13/99
RADIO UNICA COMMUNICATIONS CORP	UNCA	10/19/99	11/13/99
SATYAM INFOWAY LTD	SIFY	10/19/99	11/13/99
WORLD WRESTLING FEDERATION ENTERTAINMENT INC	WWFE	10/19/99	11/13/99
BSQUARE CORP	BSQR	10/20/99	11/14/99
CHARLOTTE RUSSE HOLDING INC	CHIC	10/20/99	11/14/99
CROSSROADS SYSTEMS INC	CRDS	10/20/99	11/14/99
ZAPMEI CORP	IZAP	10/20/99	11/14/99
AETHER SYSTEMS INC	AETH	10/21/99	11/15/99
MCK COMMUNICATIONS INC	MCKC	10/22/99	11/16/99
NAVISITE INC	NAVI	10/22/99	11/16/99
SYCAMORE NETWORKS INC	SCMR	10/22/99	11/16/99
CELANESE AG	CZ, CZ.V, CZZ	10/26/99	11/20/99

Source: Courtesy of Ostman's Alert-IPO (www.ostman.com). Used with permission.

Pollack: We provide complete coverage on IPO companies from the day they file with the SEC until they price and begin trading in public on the secondary market. In many cases, we actually cover private companies well before they file to go public such as Goldman Sachs or UPS. After the company does go public, we continue to cover them in our broader Hoover's Online business coverage, which includes a database of some 15,000 companies and organizations. Using our in-depth in-house company information and the editorially selected third-party content, we provide IPO investors with the most comprehensive research tools and the complete information to make effective investment decisions.

IPOguys: Do you target investors who invest in the "offering price," or in the "secondary market," or both?

Figure 5.8   Lockup Calendar Page

Company	Ticker	Priced	Period	Expires
APPLIED THEORY CORP	ATHY	4/30/99	180	10/27/99
GOLDMAN SACHS GROUP INC	GS	5/3/99	180	10/30/99
MAPQUEST.COM INC	MOST	5/3/99	180	10/30/99
FLYCAST COMMUNICATIONS CORP	FCST	5/4/99	180	10/31/99
SILKNET SOFTWARE INC	SILK	5/5/99	180	11/1/99
NORTHPOINT COMMUNICATIONS HOLDINGS INC	NPNT	5/5/99	180	11/1/99
PORTAL SOFTWARE INC	PRSF	5/5/99	180	11/1/99
COMPS.COM INC	CDOT	5/5/99	180	11/1/99
RADIO ONE INC	ROIA	5/5/99	180	11/1/99
DESTIA COMMUNICATIONS INC	DEST	5/6/99	180	11/2/99
LATITUDE COMMUNICATIONS INC	LATD	5/6/99	180	11/2/99
NETOBJECTS INC	NETO	5/7/99	180	11/3/99
MEDIA METRIX INC	MMXI	5/7/99	180	11/3/99
ADFORCE INC	ADFC	5/7/99	180	11/3/99
THESTREET.COM	TSCM	5/10/99	180	11/6/99
CAREERBUILDER INC	CBDR	5/11/99	180	11/7/99
MAKER COMMUNICATIONS INC	MAKR	5/11/99	180	11/7/99
TIME WARNER TELECOM INC	TWTC	5/11/99	180	11/7/99
WESCO INTERNATIONAL INC	WCC	5/11/99	180	11/7/99
INTELLIGENT LIFE CORP	ILIF	5/12/99	180	11/8/99
COPPER MOUNTAIN NETWORKS INC	CMTN	5/12/99	180	11/8/99
SCIENT CORP	SCNT	5/13/99	180	11/9/99
NEXTCARD INC	NXCD	5/14/99	180	11/10/99

Source: Courtesy of Ostman's Alert-IPO (www.ostman.com). Used with permission.

Pollack: Both. Investors who follow companies on the days they file come to us for the latest updates on changes made to the offerings, as well as to receive first word on when they actually start trading. After the debut, investors can continue to monitor their favorite IPOs through our historical stock charts, archive news links, real-time SEC filings, portfolio tools, historical financials, and many other tools found on Hoover's Online.

We also provide information for investors who are able to get in at the offering price. These users can benefit from our coverage of underwriters, offering amount, management information, pricing ranges, etc. All of this data helps investors better understand the company's position and market conditions, and the factors that may move it up or down as it begins trading.

Figure 5.9   IPO Central Page

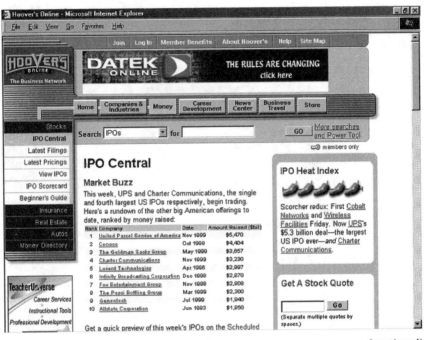

(continued)

Source: Courtesy of Hoover's Online (www.hoovers.com). Used with permission.

IPOguys: What are Hoover's plans for the future? What are your plans for the Hoover's Web site?

Pollack: Hoover's Online and IPO Central continue to grow and add more offerings. In the years ahead, we intend to expand our offerings in response to features we believe are important and to those that our users suggest.

IPOguys: What kind of effect do you see the Internet having on the IPO market and the current distribution of IPOs?

Pollack: Powerful and profound to say the least. With the Internet, there is an immeasurable amount of IPO information once relegated to high net-worth investors or institutional players that is

Figure 5.9 *(Continued)*

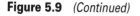

IPOs On Deck: Week of Nov. 8

Company	Symbol	Status
ASD Systems, Inc.	ASDS	
Centerprise Advisors, Inc.	CAI	
Charter Communications, Inc.	CHTR	trading
CVC, Inc.	CVCI	
Data Critical Corporation	DCCA	trading
Edison Schools, Inc.	EDSN	
Expedia, Inc.	EXPE	priced
Finisar Corporation	FNSR	
FreeMarkets, Inc.	FMKT	
iBasis, Inc.	IBAS	
Immersion Corporation	IMMR	
Intelli-Check, Inc.	IDN	
NetCreations, Inc.	NTCR	
Netzee, Inc.	NETZ	trading
Next Level Communications, Inc.	NXTV	
Pelican Financial, Inc.	PNBH	
The Plastic Surgery Company	PSU	
Quintus Corporation	QNTS	
Rudolph Technologies, Inc.	RTEC	
Sage, Inc.	SAGI	
Silicon Entertainment, Inc.	SENT	
Somera Communications, Inc.	SMPA	
SonicWALL, Inc.	SNWL	
United Parcel Service of America, Inc.	UPS	priced

IPO Alert!
Latest SEC filings
Hotel Reservations Network, Inc.
S-1, 11/9/99, 10:32 CST

Never Miss Another IPO Opportunity!
Keep up with the latest IPO offerings and notifications from selected online brokers. IPOpatrol brings you instant alerts through your e-mail, pager or cell phone. Sign up NOW!

IPO Update
Free Weekly Update From Hoover's IPO Central
Get Your E-mail Update of IPO filings, pricings, and scheduled offerings for the coming week.
Attention: Palm Pilot users Now IPO Update is available

now made available to the average investors at real or near real time. We hope that Hoover's is helping to empower this new breed of IPO investors.

IPOguys: Does your site evaluate IPOs for the IPO investor? If so, what are your guidelines?

Pollack: Not really. We don't give stock tips or provide buy/sell recommendations at our site. However, the comprehensive information found in IPO Central does allow our users to become better equipped to make those investment decisions for themselves.

Free sections available

Subscription (fee-based) service: N/A

Figure 5.10   IPO Update Page

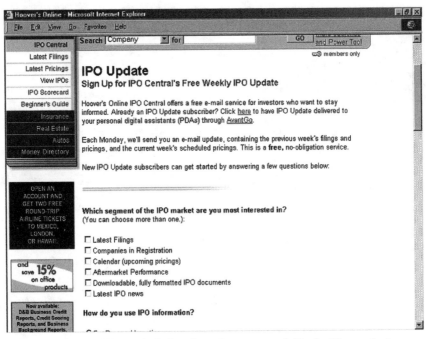

Source: Courtesy of Hoover's Online (www.hoovers.com). Used with permission.

EDGAR Online
http://www.edgar-online.com

EDGAR Online makes available for free download the most critical piece of information available to the IPO investor and the complete prospectus that has been filed with the SEC (see Figure 5.12 on page 80). They provide free complete document navigation and free download of Income Statements, Balance Sheets, and Cash Flow information into Excel or another spreadsheet application for analysis purposes. They also provide a great search tool that allows you to search the SEC database by a variety of criteria including company name, ticker, filing type, sector, industries, location, and specific date range (see Figure 5.13 on page 81). Another unique feature unique to EDGAR is their view "Today's Filings"

Figure 5.11   IPO Scorecard Page

Source: Courtesy of Hoover's Online (www.hoovers.com). Used with permission.

page, which is a free real-time list of new SEC filings as they occur. You can also research corporate management teams and boards of directors with the EDGAR Online People feature. Complex keyword searching is also available.

Free sections available

*View Complete Company Prospectus, full search of document library.

Subscription (fee-based) service: You may also sign up for the EDGAR Online Premium paid subscription service allowing RTF downloads, 144 filing access, and complete use of the EDGAR Online People service.

Figure 5.12   EDGAR Online Home Page

Copyright © by EDGAR Online, Inc. (www.edgar-online.com). Used with permission.

IPO Express
http://www.ipo-express.com

IPO Express, created by the same people that bring you EDGAR Online, provides detailed information on IPO filings, pricings, and performance. There is data on over 2,600 IPO filings and over 1,400 underwriters. Users can search by industry, company, underwriter, and geographic location. For each IPO, users are provided details on the offering, the business, financials, management, shareholders, competition, underwriters, auditors and legal counsel, and risk factors.

Free sections available

*The IPO Express Web service is completely free

Figure 5.13   EDGAR Online Search Page

Copyright © by EDGAR Online, Inc. (www.edgar-online.com). Used with permission.

Subscription (fee-based) service: IPO Express e-mail alerts for $3/month, which provide the user with daily, weekly, and nightly news and analysis about current IPOs. Also, the Now Trading service provides instant notification of when an IPO begins trading for $20/month.

FreeEDGAR
http://www.freeedgar.com

Created by EDGAR Online, FreeEDGAR is the company's value offering with free access to the SEC reports including S-1s (the IPO prospectus). Ticker- and company-based searching is available, as well as the keyword search of the SEC database.

Free sections available: Entire service is free

Subscription (fee-based) service: Entire service is free

Red Herring
http://www.redherring.com

The Red Herring site is an online version of the *Red Herring Magazine*. The Web site has four main features:

1. Insider News & Analysis
2. Herring Investor
3. Companies, Industries, and People
4. Venture Capital

This site's greatest strength is the inside look it provides of the leading technology and Internet companies, and who is investing in them. Sometimes the site rates upcoming IPOs.

Recently, the Red Herring added a section to their site (link is located near the bottom of the Web site) called the IPO Calendar, where upcoming IPOs are listed and evaluated based on a five-tiered scale known as their "Street Poll." The five tiers are cool, mild, warm, hot, and red-hot. Although a disclaimer states that the Street Poll is neither a solicitation nor recommendation, it is a good place for the IPO investor to frequent to become familiar with IPO evaluation and performance. At the IPO Calendar section, you can also look up IPO information including filings, pricings, underwriters, and withdrawals. We also found a great IPO Search tool located under the link called "Companies" where you can search for IPO information based on filters by underwriter, auditor, law firm, transfer agent, or by exchange, offering size, share type, number of shares, and number of employees.

Free sections available

Subscription (fee-based) service: N/A

CBS Marketwatch
http://cbs.marketwatch.com

This is a great free site for researching upcoming information on IPOs and for general market information. The "IPO Daily Report" and the "IPO of the Week" are the two main sections investors may want to read.

We e-mail interviewed the CEO of Marketwatch.com, Larry Kramer, and here are some of his comments.[2]

IPOguys: What do you think is the most valuable function your Web site/service provides to IPO investors?

Kramer: Information AND perspective at breaking news speed. Our daily IPO Report is the centerpiece of our public share sale service. It previews the potential hot sales, covers them as they're happening and in most cases follows them well after the rest of the media has moved on to the next big sale.

IPOguys: Do you have any other plans or ideas for the future of your Web site/business? Where do you see your company in three to five years?

Kramer: Current plans are to leverage our Web expertise into both television and radio to become the No. 1 source for financial news across all major media. Our new CBS MarketWatch Weekend TV show is reporting growing viewership across the nation and we have just started distributing our Internet reports over AOL. Over the next few years we will continue expanding over the Web and through television, with growth in Europe and Asia fast becoming a priority.

IPOguys: How is the Internet going to affect the distribution of IPOs?

Kramer: The Internet has had an historic effect on both the IPO market and the stock market in general in the last few years as hundreds of Web companies have gone public. For small investors, the offering of IPO access through W.R. Hambrecht, Wit, E-Trade and now Schwab will greatly change how shares are sold and bring more people into the market. There is a danger, however, that the newfound freedom for potential IPO investors could contribute to a stock market bubble and cost small investors dearly if the market collapses.

IPOguys: Does your site evaluate and analyze IPOs for the individual investor? If so, what are your guidelines?

Kramer: Yes. Guidelines depend on the issue and its newsworthiness. We report on what the big sales will be, how they do, and why. We also publish an IPO pick of the week, written by research firm Renaissance Capital. But we don't make our own recommendations, as it would conflict with our mandate to provide unbiased financial news coverage.

Free sections available

IPO Monitor
http://www.ipomonitor.com

This site is similar to Ostman's Alert-IPO. You can view recent IPO pricings, aftermarket performance of IPOs, and companies that have recently filed for an IPO. This is a subscription-based Web site.

Free sections available

Subscription (fee-based) service

Internet News
http://www.internetnews.com

This site is one of our favorites. The stock channel has an un-limited number of stories relating to stocks and Internet-related IPOs. Check out the IPO Report, and the morning and evening report. Tom Taulli is currently the senior Internet analyst at Internetnews.com. Sign up for the free Internet Stock newsletter sent out daily. Internet Stock News also has a subscription service called *HotWatch*. The newsletter comes monthly and highlights the top 10 Internet stocks for the month. The *HotWatch* newsletter is $99.00 a month.

Free Web site

Free daily newsletter

Subscription for monthly newsletter

IPO.com
http://www.ipo.com

IPO.com has a free e-mail registration that will send you e-mails for upcoming IPOs. You will also receive a weekly summary via e-mail with aftermarket performance and analysis. This is also a good site for learning about IPO opportunities that are sold through smaller underwriters.

Free sections available

Subscription (fee-based) service

ipoPros.com
http://www.ipoPros.com

This is a new subscription-based site that provides investors with a professional analysis and rating system of new issues (see Figure 5.14). Ben Holmes, president of ipoPros.com, believes the site provides the most in-depth analysis and pre-IPO coverage on the Web. "We actually have a professional opinion on new issues,

Figure 5.14   ipoPros.com Home Page

Source: Courtesy of ipoPros.com (www.ipoPros.com). Used with permission.

and we rank them accordingly. We're not afraid to put our name and analysis on the line for the individual investor."[3]

Free sections available

Subscription (fee-based) service

ipohome.com (Renaissance Capital)
http://www.ipohome.com

This Web site provides a nice balance of information to the IPO investor (See Figure 5.15). Most of the information is free, except for research reports, which can be downloaded for a fee. We interviewed Renaissance Capital and here is what they had to say about their company.[4]

Figure 5.15   IPOhome.com Page

Source: Courtesy of IPO.com (www.ipohome.com). Used with permission.

IPOguys: Does IPOhome.com evaluate IPOs for the IPO investor? If so, what are your guidelines?

Renaissance Capital: We evaluate every IPO. We look at four factors: (1) company fundamentals (e.g., track record, competitive positioning); (2) management and control (e.g., are management's and owners interests aligned with shareholders); (3) valuation (e.g., how the proposed price compares to the IPOs peer group); and (4) group momentum (e.g., the relative strength of the stocks in the IPOs peer group).

IPOguys: Tell us a little about your site ipohome.com.

Renaissance Capital: Thanks for identifying our site. We are the most complete, accurate, and informative IPO site. Since IPOs are at the highest end of the risk spectrum of public equity investing, we hope that individuals who use our site will become better investors. If they decide it takes too much time and attention, we offer the one and only IPO mutual fund, called the IPO Plus Aftermarket Fund (symbol IPOSX), minimum investment is $2,500.

We would like to note that the IPO Plus Aftermarket Fund for 12 months ending 11/17/99 is up 111.3 percent.

Subscription (fee-based) service

IPO Financial Network
http://IPOfinancial.com

David Menlow founded the IPO Financial Network in 1990 (see Figure 5.16). David believes that his network of services "are the premier in the IPO business. Initial Public Offerings (IPOs) have created more millionaires than any other segment of the stock market."[5] The IPO Financial Network currently consists of four main services:

1. *IPO Frontline.* A biweekly newsletter delivered via postal mail. The newsletter has been in circulation since 1998.

2. *IPOfn Telephone Network.* IPO data and information provided through your telephone.

3. *IPOfn Fax Package.* Data for the buy-side professional.

Figure 5.16   IPO Financial Network Home Page

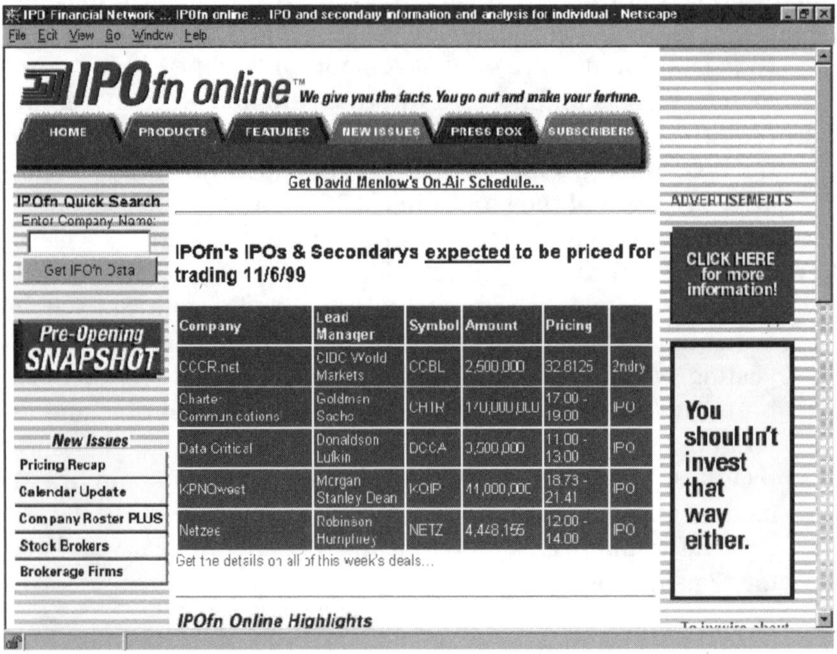

4. *IPOfn Online.* IPO data accessible through the Web. The first online product called "Pre-Opening Snapshot" is one of the best IPO services we have seen (see Figure 5.17). The "snapshot" provides traders the bid and ask price of both the "lead underwriter" and the "market makers" prior to the IPO opening. If you plan on buying IPOs in the aftermarket, this service will provide you pricing 20 to 40 minutes prior to the open. This service is a good money management tool for the online investor.

The fifth service of the IPO Financial Network MyIPOfn.com—should be available to online investors by the time of the printing of this book. At MyIPOfn.com, the user can create a personalized IPOfn

Figure 5.17   IPO Financial Network IPO Snapshot

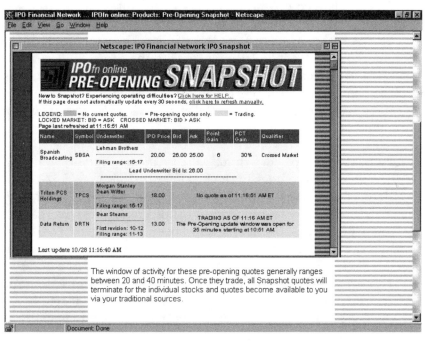

Source: Courtesy of IPO Financial Network (www.IPOfinancial.com). Used with permission.

Web page that allows the user to customize specific related IPO data to be delivered directly to that user's Web page. Users will be notified of any changes to their IPOfn Web page via an e-mail message. The user can then log in and read the content that has been delivered. Users will be able to customize data relating to any news regarding an initial public offering or secondary issue. The customized data will include buy and sell levels, IPO rankings, analysis, and any developments that take place between the time of the filing with the SEC to the effective pricing date of initial public offerings and secondary offerings. The MyIPOfn.com service will be a fee-based service.

Free and fee-based services

ipodata.com
http://www.ipodata.com

The ipodata.com Web site is one of the better research-based Web sites we have come across. This site has both free content and a subscriber-based section. You can view everything from the "Top 25 1999 IPO Weekly Price Movers" to the "Top 25 IPOs by Offering Size." You can research almost any historical data on IPOs back to the early 1990s. We e-mail interviewed the president of IPO Data Systems, Inc., John J. DeFalco, and these were some of his comments.[6]

IPOguys: What do you think is the most valuable function ipodata.com provides to the IPO investor?

DeFalco: Prospectus summary. People do not have a lot of time nowadays to research hundreds of companies by reading their prospectus from cover to cover. With our site you can research a large amount of IPOs in a short period of time. We also offer extensive search functions that investors can use to narrow the field when looking for potential investments. We do not consider ourselves a replacement for full due diligence, just a short cut to the meat of their investment research.

IPOguys: Where do you see your company in three to five years?

DeFalco: In three years we plan on to still being here offering the same high quality IPO information we always have. As technology presents itself we'll continue to bring value-added IPO services to the users of the system.

IPOguys: What kind of effect do you see the Internet having on the IPO market and the current distribution of IPOs?

DeFalco: We see the Internet opening the IPO market to the average investor. We've already seen a market change in investing with the rise of the day trader (for better or worse) and online brokerages, real-time information to e-mail/pagers/etc.

Free and subscriber-based Web site

Some other sites that are popular with IPO investors include IPOSpotlight.com, IPOMaven.com, Yahoo.com (Finance section), and WSJ.com (Wall Street Journal Online).

Information Source 3—Trade Publications

Stay on top of trends and developments within your areas of investment interest. Look for articles that allow you to focus on industry trends, and be on the lookout for companies in the best position to capitalize on these trends. Also, look for companies that are poised to secure the market leadership position by being the first to the market.

As the primary focus right now is on Internet and IPO investing, here are a few of the leading trade publications in this arena.

Red Herring
http://www.redherring.com

We rank this site number one in the area of trade expertise. Its greatest strength is that it provides an "inside look" at the leading technology and Internet companies, and who is investing in them. The Red Herring also provides a daily newsletter if you are interested in receiving daily briefings. In addition to focusing on technology and Internet start-ups, they do an excellent job at identifying evolving business models and trends. This magazine can also be found in the printed format at select stores.

Silicon Valley Investor
http://www.siliconinvestor.com (e-mail newsletter)

This is the best e-mail newsletter we could find. It provides concise, timely, and significant Internet and technology news on a daily basis.

Wall Street Journal
http://www.wsj.com

Also available online, the *Wall Street Journal* is the standard by which all trade newspapers are measured. Every Monday in the Money section of the *WSJ*, there is an IPO summary and update of the current IPO market.

Paid subscription available

Business 2.0
http://www.business2.com (Print)

This magazine is one of our favorites. *Business 2.0* does an excellent job covering the stories related to the future of business, and how it is being impacted by the Internet and modern technology. The subtitle to this magazine best describes its contents: "New Economy * New Rules * New Leaders." This magazine has received awards from the Western Publications Association, "Best New Publication, Best Special Interest Publication, and Best Overall Publication," and "from the Computer Press Association, Best Newcomer Publication, and finalist for best Overall Publication" (see Figure 5.18).[7]

Information Source 4—Venture Capitalists

What is a venture capitalist? A venture capitalist is a company or person that invests cash in a start-up company in exchange mainly for equity or stock issued by the start-up. The venture capitalist is betting, or risking that the investment up front in the early stage of development will pay off when the start-up goes public or gets acquired. The venture capitalists' payoff, or return on their investment, is targeted to be at least 10 times the original investment. Venture capital firms were traditionally formed to provide investment opportunities for large institutional companies like universities and state governments. These institutions would fund the venture capital firms to invest in start-ups. You ask, "Why would a conservative institution like a university want to take such a risk?" The reason is that in any balanced investment portfolio there should be some portion of risk. This portion was generally very low; thus the universities could take a little risk with a chance of large rewards. The investment was a hedge against their conservative investments like bonds.

Today, the typical venture capital firm is changing in the way it generates money. Many VC firms are raising cash for investments from individuals. The Internet revolution has made thousands of millionaires and many billionaires. Many of these wealthy individuals are investing their money in venture capital firms. Still, the majority of money raised by venture capitalists comes from the traditional large institutions like state governments, insurance companies, pension funds, or universities.

A high-tech start-up needs cash for many reasons: Currently, the main ones are to advertise and market their product or service, and to hire key employees. In exchange for the cash, the venture

Figure 5.18   *Business 2.0* Magazine Cover

Source: Reprinted with permission from *Business 2.0: www.business2.com* © 2000 Imagine Media, Inc. *Business 2.0* is the magazine of business in the Internet Age.

capitalist will acquire a percentage of the company and will own a portion of the start-up (anywhere from 3 percent to 40 percent). Generally, the VC will get a seat on the board of directors, and sometimes even insist on participation in the hiring of future management.

The start-up has a proven business model, it is generating revenue, the management is in place; now the only thing left to do is to go public. As discussed earlier, the main reason a start-up goes public is to raise cash to grow the business.

In a way, individual investors who buy the initial public offering are just like a venture capitalist, in that they are taking ownership of a start-up prior to the company actually trading publicly on a stock exchange. The main difference is that individual investors are making much smaller investments and for a shorter period of time prior to trading on the market. Generally after the purchase, the new issue starts trading the very next day on one of the exchanges.

We hope this helps you get a feel for the overall interactive process of venture capitalists and start-ups. When deciding to invest in an IPO, look at what if any venture capital firms have an initial investment in the upcoming IPO. Who are the original investors? Is the majority investor a big-time venture capital firm like Kleiner Perkins Caufield & Byers?

We have included five of the top venture capital firms in the country. These firms have invested early on in some of the world's best high-tech start-ups.

Kleiner Perkins Caufield & Byers
http://www.kpcb.com

Since 1972, KPCB has been investing in start-ups. KPCB has funded over 100 companies and expects to invest in 80 more in the near future. KPCB was an original investor in Amazon.com. You can view their most recent investments at their Web site. Click on "Recent News" then click on "Recent Investments."

Accel Partners
http://www.accel.com

Accel is one of the leading venture capital firms in the country. Accel invested in Foundry Networks, Agile Software, Quokka Sports, RedBack Networks, Northpoint Communications, and Mpath

Interactive (now HearMe-HEAR). All these high-tech companies went public in 1999. You can see the most recent investments from Accel under the "News" link.

Benchmark Capital
http://www.benchmark.com

Benchmark Capital has invested in some of the largest first-day Internet IPO gainers ever. Benchmark invested in Ebay, Red Hat Software, and Juniper Networks. Click on "Portfolio companies" to see what companies they have invested in, plus new start-ups that may be going public in the near future.

Draper Fisher Jurvetson
http://www.drapervc.com

DFJ invested in Netzero and Wit Capital Group, which both went public in 1999. The IPOguys owned the initial offering shares in both Netzero and Wit Capital. Other current investments are in Fogdog Sports, Netcentives, Garage.com, and Direct Hit. You can view DFJ's current investments at the "Current Portfolio" link their Web page.

Sequoia Capital
http://www.sequoiacap.com

Sequoia has invested in some great companies that went public. The IPO successes include Etoys, MP3.com, Yahoo, Cisco Systems, and Oracle. Sequoia has been investing in start-ups since 1972. They are one of the leading venture capital firms in the United States. You can view current and past investments by clicking on the "Investment" link.

These are just a few of the leading venture capital firms we have highlighted. You can use the following list for additional research:

Sutter Hill Ventures	http://www.shv.com
Softbank Venture Capital	http://www.sbvc.com
Sierra Ventures	http://www.sierraven.com
Patricof & Co. Ventures, Inc.	http://www.patricof.com
Menlo Ventures	http://www.menloventures.com

Greylock	http://www.greylock.com
Crosspoint Venture Partners	http://www.cpvp.com
@Ventures	http://www.cmgi.com/@ventures /index.html
Brentwood Venture Capital	http://www.brentwoodvc.com
Bessemer Venture Partners	http://www.bessemervp.com

Information Source 5—Internet and IPO Analysts

Internet analysts' views and commentary can help increase your knowledge base about companies going public and also companies that are already trading in the aftermarket. Technology and information-based companies were developed and built at an increasing speed in 1999. Almost every other day, a new technology, software tool, or business model is being brought to the market in one way or another. Individual investors need to keep apace with this activity and new knowledge being created in the Internet economy.

Good Internet analysts are hard to come by. Not only do you have to be technically proficient, but you also need to have a vision of what the future will hold. While we are sure that there are many other good Internet analysts in addition to ones on our list, these are a few of our favorites. We have included their Web sites or the Web site they currently write for, along with a brief description about their services. Their free reports, newsletters, and articles could lead you to the next eBay. You can't listen to everyone, but it helps occasionally to listen, learn, then make your own investment decision.

Tom Taulli
http://www.taulli.com

Tom Taulli is the Internet stock analyst at internet.com (INTM). He writes a daily column for internet.com, as well as a weekly column on IPOs for CBS MarketWatch. Taulli covers most of the sectors in high tech, although, on occasion, he will cover more traditional stocks, so long as there is a high-tech connection (e.g., the UPS IPO).

In evaluating IPOs, Taulli looks for companies that have (1) strong management; (2) a business model that is sustainable in the long term; (3) a market that is fast-growing and big enough to support a public company; (4) big backers, such as top VCs like Kleiner, Benchmark, and Sequoia; (5) proven success (say a product in the marketplace); (6) some type of barriers to entry, which could even mean first-mover advantage; and (7) top underwriters/advisers.

For the next few years, he is very bullish on infrastructure and business-to-business e-commerce companies, such as Ariba, Commerce One, Juniper Networks, CacheFlow, and Sycamore Networks. Tom also has his own Web site at the link provided with his name (see Figure 5.19). Here you can buy his book called *Investing in IPOs*. Tom has a free newsletter you can subscribe to at the site.

Figure 5.19   The Taulli Report

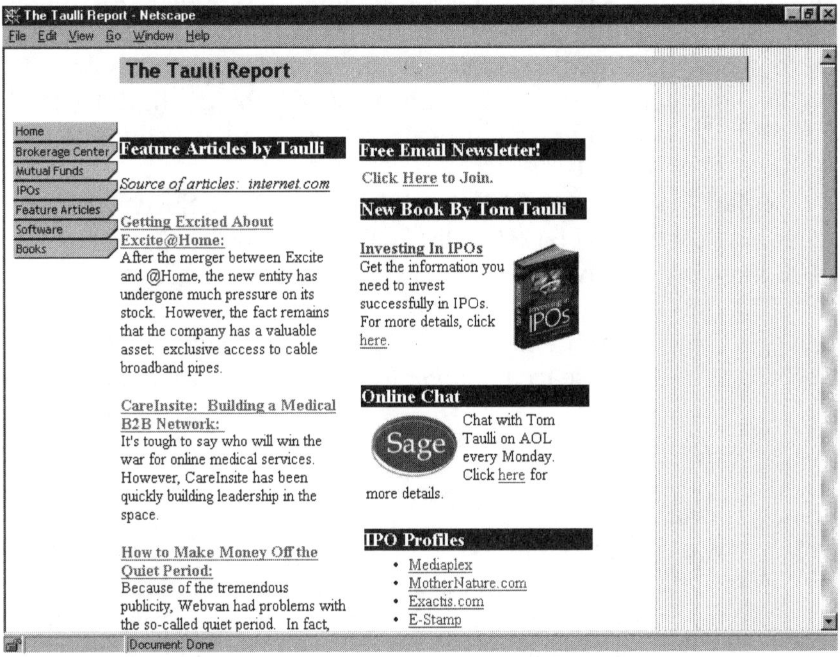

Source: Courtesy of Tom Taulli (www.taulli.com). Used with permission.

Every Monday, you can tune into AOL to hear Tom talk about IPOs. Tom also posts his featured articles on his Web site for online investors to read.[8]

Dr. Irv DeGraw (WorldFinanceNet.com)
http://www.WorldFinanceNet.com

"WFN's Research Director is Irv DeGraw. Dr. DeGraw is a nationally recognized authority on the valuation and performance of emerging industries and businesses (IPOs). He is frequently referenced by *Barron's, Bridge News, Reuters, Dow Jones,* the *Wall Street Journal,* and other industry-leading publications as well as Internet publications RedHerring.com, MSN.com, and CNBC.com, among others. He is also a syndicated columnist for the *IPO Reporter* and *On Wall Street* magazine.

Dr. DeGraw has conducted fundamental analyses of more than 2,000 companies and has specialized expertise in technology and emerging industries" (see Figure 5.20).[9]

The feature we like best on WFN is the analysis reports located in the "IPO Corner." The weekly analysis reports provide investors with a listing of the upcoming IPOs, an overall summary of the business on the featured issuing company, a financial view, and finally a prediction of where the IPO may open on the first day trading. The report also has an aftermarket trading level estimate (see Figure 5.21 on page 100).

Other sections within the IPO Corner worth viewing are "Breaking Events," "Market Pulse," "WFN Newsletter," and the link to "Education on Buying IPOs."

This site is one of the better resources currently on the Web. Much of the research and information can be attributed to Dr. Irv DeGraw, the head research analyst for WorldFinanceNet.com.

Free Web site

Francis Gaskins
http://www.gaskinsco.com

Francis Gaskins is the founder of Gaskins IPO Desktop. Gaskins IPO Desktop has a few unique IPO indexes and IPO rating systems for the online individual investor (see Figure 5.22 on page 101).

Figure 5.20   WorldFinanceNet Home Page

Source: Courtesy of Irv DeGraw and WorldFinanceNet.com (www.WorldFinanceNet .com). Used with permission.

Gaskins IPO Desktop has four main services:

1. *Gaskins IPO Value Index*™. The IPO market cap divided by prior quarter's sales. Lower is better.

2. *Rated*[1] *IPO Calendar.* The only IPO calendar with pre-IPO ratings of a company's business model. Most pre-IPO rankings are rated on Wall Street as either Hot or Cold. Gaskins ranks his IPOs based on their business model. His ranking system is unique. This is another ranking system investors can use to cross-reference an IPO's potential for not only the short term but also the long term.

Figure 5.21   WorldFinanceNet—IPO Corner

Company	Symbol	Shares	Range	Lead Underwriter
OpenTV	OPTV	7.5 million	$18-$20	Merrill Lynch

Digital interactive TV software

Interactive TV is shaping up to be one of the next major technology battlegrounds. Interactive digital set top boxes are expected to grow from 16 million in '98 to 34 million in '01, and related e-Commerce revenues are forecast in the $11 billion range by '04. So the stakes are high. On one side is Microsoft and the Windows-CE operating system. On the other is everybody else. OpenTV is one of the first direct entrants in this battle. Now, this firm is the only player with actual deployments and operations. While others are still planning, this firm has 4.3 million set top boxes in actual operation with 22 operators in 17 countries. Using the standard, familiar remote "clicker", consumers may conduct e-Commerce and banking transactions through their TV.

The technology is also attractive. Because this is a software based solution, it is compatible with existing hardware. So conversion is relatively straight forward and cheap. Operators are not required to replace expensive equipment. It is also already capable of offering such services as video on demand, once operators sufficiently boost bandwidth. It is also already compatible with digital TVs.

The firm is growing at a 184.7% rate with 1999 revenues forecast in the $24 million range. That's OK but not as impressive as the firm's investors. OpenTV is also partially owned by AOL, Sun Microsystems, News Corp., Time Warner, General Instrument (a set top box maker), and Liberty Digital. Its scope is also worldwide. With investors of this caliber, the offering is sure to receive high profile market attention. Pre-offering demand is already reported as strong and expected to intensify into the IPO. Expect a 100+% first day followed by near term appreciation.

Source: Courtesy of Irv DeGraw and WorldFinanceNet.com (www.WorldFinanceNet .com). Used with permission.

Business Model Rating Criteria:
A = high growth market, potential leader
B = more competitive market
C = public venture capital

3. *Pre-IPO Ratings.* Includes prior fourth-quarter's results for sales, gross margin, profit/loss plus business model comments. Source: SEC filings plus industry knowledge.

4. *IPO P&L Scorecard.* Compares first-day IPO high with the weekend Friday's close. Most of the services at Gaskins IPO Desktop are free, although he does have a few subscriber-based reports for sale.[10]

Free and subscriber-based

Figure 5.22   Gaskins IPO Desktop Page

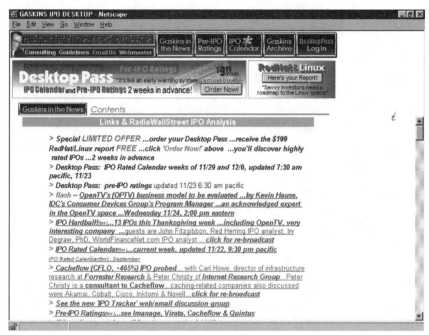

Source: Courtesy of Francis Gaskins (www.gaskinsco.com).

Rob Zimmer, Director (RadioWallStreet.com)
http://www.vcall.com
http://www.radiowallstreet.com
http://www.investorbroadcast.com

IPO Hardball is a weekly "real-time audio" interview session on RadioWallStreet.com with many of the IPO analysts we highlight in our book (Figure 5.23). IPO Hardball is heard every Monday at 4:00 P.M. EST. You can tune in right through your computer and listen to analysis and discussion of the upcoming IPOs for that week. There is also generally a summary of the past week's IPOs and their performance.

We interviewed Rob Zimmer of RadioWallStreet.com to learn what this service is all about.[11]

Figure 5.23   RadioWallStreet IPO Tracker Channel

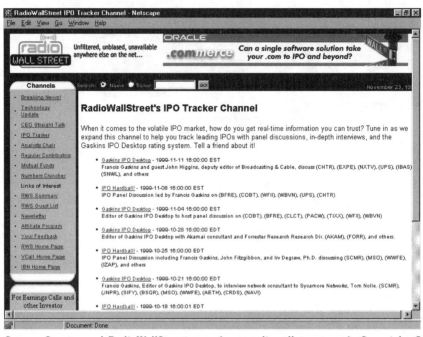

Source: Courtesy of RadioWallStreet.com (www.radiowallstreet.com). Copyright ©
by Investor Broadcast Network. All rights reserved. Used with permission.

IPOguys: Briefly, describe RadioWallStreet.com.

Zimmer: RadioWallStreet, is part of the Investor Broadcast Network, which seeks to bring timely, in-depth streaming audio financial news, analysis, and information to our registered user
base of 375K individual investors and professional analysts.

IPOguys: How can RadioWallStreet help online IPO investors?

Zimmer: Simply put, individual investors gain access to information previously available only to professionals. The VCall service provides earnings calls and shareholder information.
(VCall has exclusive Internet broadcast rights to Microsoft
calls.) The RadioWallStreet site highlights top management,

Wall Street analysts, and weekly contributor shows on leading-edge equities and sectors. We aim to bring "unbiased, unfiltered" information to the investors, who can then do their own homework and make their own best decisions. In addition, some of our most popular shows integrate audio with text links on our site—almost like "going to school" for our audience members.

IPOguys: RadioWallStreet is a very unique service. What value does it provide the online investor?

Zimmer: We provide the best available technology, a public service for investors and analysts—we tell it straight, no hidden agendas. Our IPO shows are not only very informative, but Francis Gaskins (co-host) and I do not trade the stocks—where else can investors get this kind of unbiased information?

IPOguys: What segments of the overall financial markets does Investorbroadcast.com cover?

Zimmer: Internet, semiconductor, pharmaceutical, software, Internet infrastructure, and technology stocks, with some coverage of traditional industry.

IPOguys: Do you have any other services in mind for the future?

Zimmer: We'll be integrating into the video market, also syndicating to traditional and non-traditional media. And expanding our regular shows to probe institutional and insider buying and selling trends.

Don't miss IPO Hardball!

Free service

John Fitzgibbon
http://www.redherring.com

John Fitzgibbon is a nationally recognized IPO analyst who writes for Redherring.com. "I went to work on a syndicate desk in 1973 underwriting and selling stocks, bonds, and IPOs in 1973 and was a syndicate manager for 13 years." Last year, CBS News ran a poll to determine who is/was "The Best of Wall Street" in their given specialty and recognized John for coverage of the IPO market.[12]

There seems to be a shortage these days of qualified expert IPO analysts. We have highlighted a few for our readers, but we are sure we have not included all of them. Please go to the IPOguys.com Web site for an updated listing of IPO analysts.

Summary

- Understand your personal investing tendencies. Two major factors are how much money you have, and how much money you are willing to commit to a volatile IPO market. Two additional considerations are knowing whether your gut can withstand market volatility and whether you will be overanxious to trade.

- Use IPO preinvesting strategies prior to making any IPO investments. First, be sure to diversify your portfolio to spread out your overall risk and exposure. Also, paper trade prior to investing real dollars so that you can gain some understanding and experience.

- The prospectus is an overall blueprint of the company going public and undoubtedly one of the best information sources available to the IPO investor. Before investing in any IPO, be very comfortable with the information contained therein.

- Review and analyze the prospectus (or preliminary prospectus) in detail. Look for factors that typically equate to high-performing IPOs, as well as factors that put up the warning flag for IPO disasters. There is no substitute for detailed and thorough research and analysis.

- Use the wealth of free information that is available over the Internet to help you in your IPO investing research.

- Read trade publications to stay on top of investment trends, new technologies, and business developments within your areas of interest.

- Research what, if any, venture capital firms were early investors in the start-up.

- Learn from the leading IPO analysts.

chapter 6

getting started

the step-by-step guide to purchasing ipos online

Open an Online Brokerage Account

The first step in successfully obtaining IPOs at the offering price is to open an online brokerage account with a company that offers IPOs to the individual investor. If you are trying to choose an online brokerage firm, we highly recommend Wit Capital (Web site located at http://www.witcapital.com)—the pioneer in the field of offering IPOs to the retail investor. *Kiplinger's* July 1999 issue highlighted Wit Capital in an article titled "What You Can Do with $1,000." *Kiplinger's* number one suggestion was to open an account with Wit Capital (at the time of the writing of this book, Wit Capital is requiring $2,000 to open an account). In Chapter 7, we cover Wit Capital, as well as many other online brokerage firms that offer IPOs to the individual investor in greater detail.

Research, Research, Research

There is no substitute for thoroughly researching your potential investment. Prior to investing, be sure that you are confident in the company you are looking to buy. Being selective is critical, especially to the first-time IPO buyer.

Placing a Conditional Offer

You have found a new initial public offering that you may want to purchase. You have read the prospectus and thoroughly researched the company. You are now ready to jump in and purchase your first 100 shares online. The first step toward owning the initial shares in the new offering is to place a "conditional offer" with the online investment bank. This is your "indication of interest" in buying IPO shares in a specific initial offering. Most online investment banks require conditional offers to be placed online, although a few of them will accept indications of interest over the phone.

After logging into your online brokerage account, you may make the conditional offer online by filling out the required forms. The forms are quite similar from one online investment bank to the next, and also fairly simple to fill out. You will then need to state the number of shares you want to purchase (a 100-share minimum is typical), and the price per share you are willing to pay. You also must select to purchase the shares at the "offering price" or at a "limit price." If you place a conditional offer at the offering price, you are committing to buy the shares at whatever price the underwriters set.

Most online investment banks have a window of time within which they receive conditional offers. Typically, once this time period ends, you may not be allowed to place indications of interest in the specified IPO.

When you place an indication of interest, you will find that the IPO price is often listed in a price range, rather than at a specific price. A price range is set because it is difficult to determine the level of demand for the IPO prior to accepting conditional offers. Usually the price range has a two- to three-dollar spread (sample price range: $12 to $14 per share). Sometimes the price range will change from what was originally announced, depending on the demand for the offering. If the demand for the new issue far exceeds the supply, the underwriter will often raise the price range. Conversely, the underwriters will lower the price range if the demand is soft.

To protect yourself from overpaying for an IPO due to price increases, you can set a "limit price" with the online investment bank, which is the maximum price you would be willing to pay for the shares. If the lead underwriter prices the issue higher than that price, you will not be sold the shares. Anytime before the lead underwriter sets the final price on the new issue (known as pricing), you can cancel your conditional offer or indication of interest if you decide not to participate in the offering. There is no penalty for canceling a conditional offer.

Pricing Set by the Underwriter

Although this step is one over which you have absolutely no control, it is of great importance to the individual investor. Once the new issue has been "priced" or "the price has been set" by the underwriter and the issuing company, the stock/new issue will begin trading publicly on the stock market, generally the next morning. Most of the technology and Internet IPOs are being listed on the NASDAQ exchange, while blue-chip stocks tend to be listed on the Dow Jones Industrial Average. Generally, the pricing of the new issue is set by the lead underwriter in the evening between 4:00 P.M. and 9:00 P.M. (EST).

When an IPO prices, most online investment banks may require you to "reconfirm" your conditional offer in the offering. Most online investment banks will notify investors that an IPO has been priced via e-mail or by phone. Once you reconfirm with the investment bank, your conditional offer becomes an executable buy order.

Most online investment banks require investors to reconfirm their conditional offer when the shares price. The banks usually send out e-mail confirmations between 5:30 P.M. and 8:30 P.M. (EST) on the night when the IPO officially prices. Investors who do not reconfirm their original conditional offer will not receive shares in the offering.

E*TRADE and fbr.com are the only companies we know of that currently do not require you to reconfirm your indication of interest the day the IPO prices, unless the offering price or range has been changed. Instead, E*TRADE requires you to confirm your original conditional offer by completing a form that states conditional offers placed and not canceled prior to the time of pricing will be considered valid.

After you reconfirm either by e-mail or by phone, an online investment bank will contact you again to notify you whether you have been "allocated" shares. Shares are allocated to individual investors either on a first-come, first-serve basis, or through a lottery format. In Chapter 7, we list the different online investment banks that offer IPOs to individual investors, and the current allocation rules and procedures.

If you have been allocated shares, you generally receive an e-mail stating the number of shares that will be deposited into your account, and the date at which you must pay for the shares, referred to as the "settlement date." Most of the online investment banks will want to receive full payment for the shares within 3 to 5 days after the pricing of the new issue. The shares may not show up visibly in your account until 24 hours after the pricing of the new issue.

Even though you've confirmed your conditional offer/indication of interest, this does not mean that you have a guarantee to receive any shares. In fact, it is pretty safe to assume that every individual IPO investor will experience the frustration of not being allocated shares at some point in his or her IPO investing career. With a good IPO strategy, you may be able to obtain many hot IPOs that you seek, but even with the best strategies in place, you may face the day when you are not allocated shares in the IPO of your choice.

No Shares?

Our suggestion to the individual investor who is not allocated shares is to get over it and move on! If you can't develop this mentality, then you have the IPO market out of perspective. Remember, there are many investors with millions of dollars in traditional brokerage accounts who aren't even getting the chance to purchase the IPOs that the individual investor has access to. Keep your chin up and move on. Don't become discouraged because you didn't get a particular IPO. Instead, focus your time and efforts on finding the IPOs you are going to target next. The hot IPOs tend to be in extremely scarce supply. Be patient, be persistent, and most importantly, continue to be selective.

You Are Allocated Shares, Now What?

You now have shares in your first initial public offering. What to do . . . oh what to do. . . . Here are some possible IPO investing strategies.

Strategy 1: Flipping

One strategy you can follow in IPO investing is to buy every IPO you can get your hands on and then sell on the first day, capitalizing on the immediate gain often experienced on the first day of trading. Also known as "flipping," selling on the first day is completely legal, but often discouraged by most online investment banks we highlight in the book. Some firms penalize you for flipping by excluding you from future offerings, for a limited period. This strategy is important because it is sometimes wise to take your profits, even if it means going through a 60- or 90-day penalty period where you may not be allocated shares. This is especially true when an IPO "moonshots," or jumps 100 percent or more in the first day of trading.

While we do not encourage flipping, we also do not discourage it. The individual investor needs to weigh the consequences of being excluded from future offerings and decide to flip or not to flip. Our advice? If you're going to flip with a investment bank that will penalize you for it, flip on a moonshot to make it worthwhile since it may be quite a while before your next IPO. If you have difficulty making quick decisions, set price targets for your stocks so that the stock automatically sells when it reaches a certain price. Setting an order to sell at a specified price target is known as setting a limit order.

We typically try to hold onto our initial shares for a minimum of 30 to 75 days to avoid penalties imposed by some online investment banks for selling too soon. It is difficult to pass on the opportunity to make a quick, short-term gain, and occasionally we have capitalized on moonshots. We also remind ourselves of the golden rule: Never be afraid to take a profit. This is especially true in a market filled with volatility, since the tides can turn against you just as quickly as they turned in your favor. A profitable trade, even if it has to be a flip, is "money in the bank." We have seen profits turn into losses by investors who fear being penalized for flipping. Taking profit is also especially important for your first IPO trade. Having profit to reinvest should make it easier for you to withstand market fluctuations of future IPO purchases that you decide to hold for the long term. If you end up being penalized for flipping by an online investment bank and have difficulty getting shares, you might want to consider transferring your money to another online investment bank that will give you shares and then move your money back when the penalty period is over. Although we have never tried this, it might be worth looking into.

Strategy 2: Holding for the Long Term
The next strategy in IPO investing would be to hold the IPOs for the long term. This strategy truly requires an iron gut, especially when investing in highly volatile hot sectors, such as the Internet.

The "holding for the long term" strategy is a good one to follow if Ben Holmes, president of ipoPros.com, is accurate in his assessment that "as the e-underwriters mature and increase their client base, they will become more selective in who they allocate shares to. Just as the current Brick & Mortar investment banks allocate IPOs to their best clients, the e-underwriters will want good accounts, not just flippers, or clients that only buy IPOs."[1]

What is the outlook for the buy-and-hold strategy? No one knows for sure how long the IPO market as a whole will continue to perform at such incredible levels. Internet and computer technology are two areas currently driving the market, and the future in these areas looks bright. Even if the bull market were to end, many future Microsofts and eBays are inevitably going to be born and emerge. The possibility of investing in these young companies should continue to attract capital to the IPO market. So, even if the Internet IPO mania ends, there will always be companies that succeed in the IPO market and provide the IPO investor with excellent opportunities.

"Although comparisons are difficult, the average return on all IPOs brought to market in the 1990s is 106 percent CommScan says."[2]

Strategy 3: Buy after the Moonshot Collapse

Another good strategy in IPO investing may be to wait for the initial mania and high trading activity surrounding the moonshot IPOs to settle down, then buy. Following this strategy will sometimes allow the IPO investor to buy shares of a highly desired IPO at a very reasonable price. On occasion, you may even be able to buy the IPO at a price equal to or below the offering price. It is difficult to time this properly, especially on your first attempt. The most common mistake investors make with this strategy is not waiting long enough. Our trading experience has shown us that usually it takes at least two weeks for the hype surrounding an IPO to settle and may take two to three months.

Strategy 4: Short-Sell a Moonshot

This requires a margin account, which allows you to leverage your assets in the account. Short-selling requires a true iron gut in a bull market, and allows many investors to make a killing in a bear market. If you plan on short-selling a moonshot, be sure the bubble has popped before investing in. It is usually wise to wait a couple of days before short-selling an IPO because sometimes there is life in the IPO for two to three days after the initial craze. Personally, we have avoided short-selling, but mention it for the "bearish" investor.

Strategy 5: Be Prepared for Significant Dates

Be prepared for significant dates such as the end of the "quiet period" and the end of the "lockups." These dates often impact the movement of the stock price. You can stay on top of these dates by reviewing the various IPO Web sites, or by using some of the tools described later in this book.

In the past, traders were able to benefit from the rise and fall in the stock price and to make profits by buying and selling just a few days prior to these dates. However, more individual investors are wising up to the causes of price fluctuations, and time frames may enlarge as investors attempt to make their trades before everyone else.

The Quiet Period   After a new issue starts trading, the company and other underwriters are not allowed by SEC regulations to promote or provide recommendations for 25 days after the first day of trading. Generally, the stock is said to be in the "quiet period" during this time. After the 25 days are over, the underwriters, the company, and any other analysts can comment or give public buy or sell recommendations on the company. The quiet period allows the new stock price to stabilize and hold in a general range following the initial shares sold to the public. Many times a good company will moonshot after the 25-day quiet period is over. Ebay was a good example of this scenario.

Lockups   When a company goes public, the major shareholders (who are usually the corporate officers) are often restricted from selling their shares for a predetermined period, generally a minimum of 6 months, although we have seen this trend changing to even shorter time limitations. This time freeze is referred to as the "lockup" period and is established to discourage selling by the major shareholders and to help provide stability in the stock price. Many times the price may fall just prior to the end of a lockup period as investors fear a sell-off. Conversely, if the major shareholders don't sell and decide to hold their stock positions after the lockup period has expired, this may boost investors' confidence in the stock, causing prices to rise.

In Chapter 7, we discuss the different online investment banks that are working to level the playing field for individual investors by allowing them to obtain shares in some of the hottest IPOs around.

Summary

- Set up an account with Wit Capital or one of the other online investment banks that offer IPOs to the individual investor. We cover online investment banks in greater detail in Chapter 7.

- Monitor your e-mail and the Web page. Place a conditional offer after you have researched and read the prospectus of the new issue.

- Reconfirm your conditional offer in an IPO if required by the online brokerage firm.

- Once you are allocated shares, be prepared and ready to act or not act depending on the performance of the IPO.

- Know your five main IPO investing strategies: flipping, buying and holding for the long term, buying after the moonshot collapse, short-selling a moonshot, and being prepared for specific dates. Apply these strategies to every IPO on an individual basis, depending on the performance of the IPO.

- Set price targets (ranges) to help you make quick and decisive buy or sell decisions. If you are going to flip, make sure it is worth your while since you may be penalized from receiving future allocations for a period of time.

chapter 7

where to buy ipos

online investment firms offering ipos to individual investors

Here we outline the top nine online investment banks that provide IPOs to individual investors. The Internet is breaking new ground, and for the first time in the history of the IPO process, individual investors have the opportunity to buy shares at the initial share price. We salute these nine companies as pioneers in the financial industry.

We list each firm, discuss each company briefly, and describe the process investors need to go through to open an account. We also highlight a few key tips about each company.

Procedures and processes will have changed from one online investment bank to another by the time this book is published and printed, but the following material can serve as a guide for online individual investors. Our guidelines are based on information as of November 1, 1999.

Top Online Investment Banks

Wit Capital Group
http://www.witcapital.com

Wit Capital is currently the primary leader in the market of providing IPOs to individual investors (see Figure 7.1). We began following Wit Capital in July 1998 and purchased our first IPO from them in January 1999.

It is fairly easy to register and open an account by applying online, and then printing out and mailing in the application. We highly recommend you visit Wit Capital's

Figure 7.1   Wit Capital Home Page

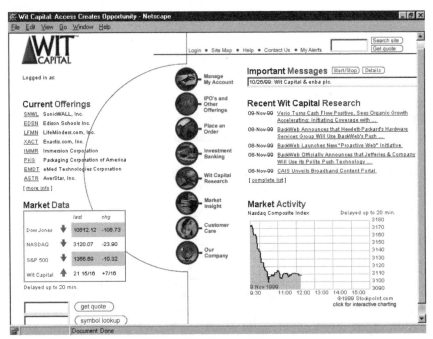

Source: Courtesy of Wit Capital (www.witcapital.com). Used with permission.

guide to "Participating in IPO's and Other Offering" (see Figure 7.2). The tour walks you through the entire process of purchasing IPOs. This new feature is the best tutorial we have seen yet from any of the online investment banks.

At the end of the application process, you will be assigned an account number and a User ID. You will also need to deposit a minimum $2,000 into your account. When new IPOs become available for indications of interest, Wit Capital sends out e-mails called "IPO Alerts" to all account holders informing them of the new offering. You can also view new IPO offerings at the "Current Offerings" page (see Figure 7.3). Interested investors can then proceed to the appropriate Web page to place indications of interest and to read the prospectus.

Figure 7.2   Your Guide to Using Wit Capital

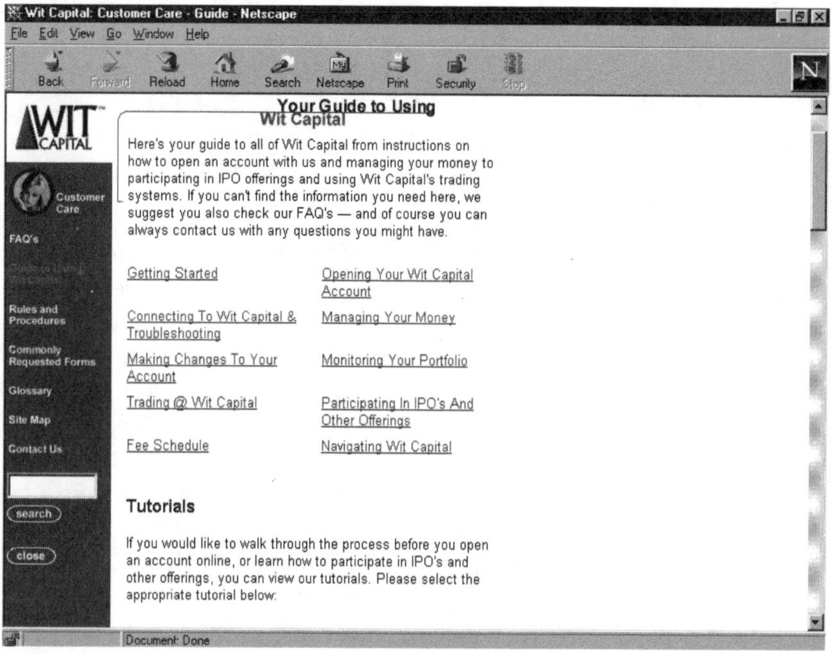

Source: Courtesy of Wit Capital (www.witcapital.com). Used with permission.

Figure 7.3   Current Offerings Page

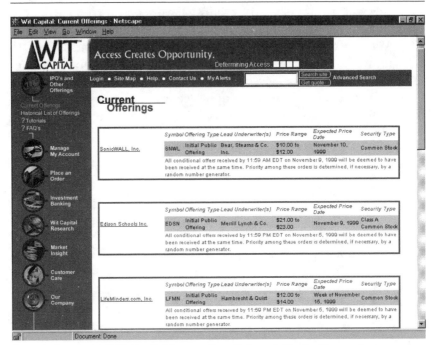

Source: Courtesy of Wit Capital (www.witcapital.com). Used with permission.

To buy shares in a new issue, you must place a conditional offer for shares. When an IPO prices for which you have made a conditional offer, Wit Capital will e-mail you asking you to reconfirm that you want to buy shares. A "conditional offer" is an offer to purchase the "new issue." When the new issue has been "declared effective" by the SEC, you must reconfirm your original conditional offer (see Figures 7.4–7.10).

When you reconfirm your offer, you will be asked to reply by typing the words "I Confirm" in the subject heading. At this point if you decide to *not* buy the IPO, then you need do nothing; the original conditional offer will be automatically canceled. If you decide to reconfirm and buy the IPO, you are still not guaranteed shares in the allocation.

Figure 7.4 Initial Public Offering Page

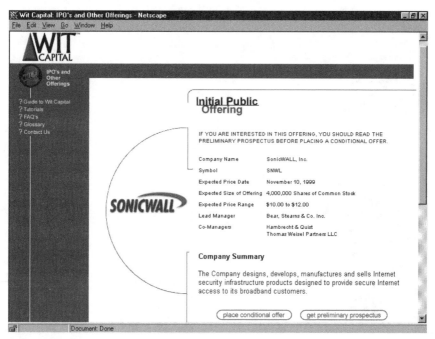

Source: Courtesy of Wit Capital (www.witcapital.com). Used with permission.

Wit Capital allocates (or sells) shares to individual investors on a modified first-come, first-serve basis for those who have placed conditional offers before the equal standing time. Shares are generally allocated in increments of 100. If you place your original conditional offer during the equal standing period, you will have equal standing (think of being tied for first) with other Wit Capital accountholders "who are in good standing," (nonflippers). If there are not enough shares for all the members who are tied for first and in good standing, then the allocations are determined by a "random number generator" (i.e., lottery). All flippers are automatically sent to the end of the line. Again please see Wit Capital's guide, "Participating in IPO's and Other Offerings."

If shares are left to allocate after all members tied for first have received allocations, then the rest of the shares will be allocated to

Figure 7.5   Offering Registration Page

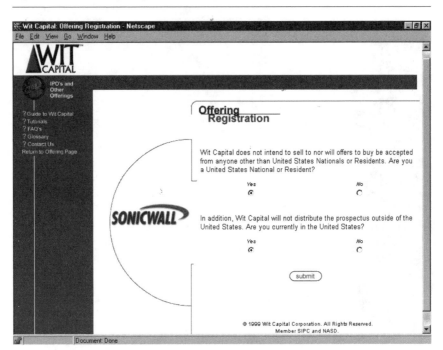

Source: Courtesy of Wit Capital (www.witcapital.com). Used with permission.

other members. Good standing members who did not place conditional offers by the equal standing time will be allocated next, followed by all the flippers, if there are any shares left to be allocated.

Investors receive back an e-mail generally between 12:30 A.M. and 7:30 A.M. (EST) the morning after notifying them whether they have been allocated shares. The shares should show up in your account under the "View Positions" section of "Manage My Account" (see Figure 7.11 on page 126). If you want to sell your shares on the first day of trading, you can sell your shares in the "trade" section under "Manage My Account." Wit Capital houses an online brokerage division. Your online account not only allows you to buy and sell IPOs, but you can also buy and sell stocks, bonds, and mutual funds (see Figure 7.12 on page 127). Wit Capital currently charges

Figure 7.6   Read the Prospectus Page

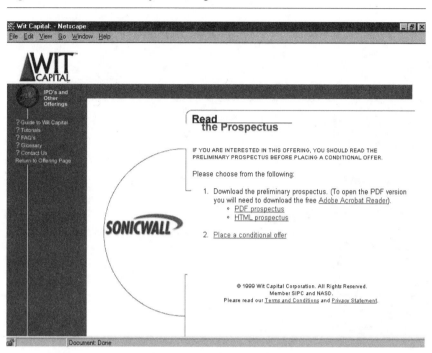

Source: Courtesy of Wit Capital (www.witcapital.com). Used with permission.

$14.95 for market orders, and $19.95 for all other orders, including limit orders, as of October 28, 1999.

Wit Capital's Web site has six main sections or links. "Current Offerings," is where IPOs are posted and where investors place conditional offers. Here the "Current Offerings" are listed in order of sequence. You can view the "new issue," see who the main underwriter is, what the price range is, and what the expected date is for pricing the new issue. You can then click on the new issue and go directly to the page, where you can place a conditional offer and read the prospectus.

"Manage My Account" allows accountholders to view their balance, positions, open orders, and trading activity. The "Open orders" page provides accountholders the ability to view both conditional

Figure 7.7   Verification Page

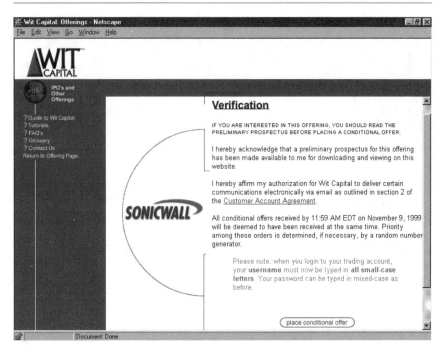

Source: Courtesy of Wit Capital (www.witcapital.com). Used with permission.

offers and any regular stock holdings. It also allows users to change or cancel a conditional offer.

"Place Orders" is where investors can buy and sell securities online. This is where they also sell any IPO allocations they have received. Make sure you review the "Trading @ Wit Capital" page to learn how to correctly buy and sell securities.

"Research Analysis" provides investors with institutional quality investments reports on publicly traded Internet companies. Analyst Jonathan Cohen and his team of approximately 50 (and growing) analysts write most of the research reports. Click on the "Valuation Matrix" to get an idea of how Wit Capital analysts value present Internet companies. There is also a valuable "Research Tutorial" that will help you understand and analyze the research

Figure 7.8   Conditional Offer Page

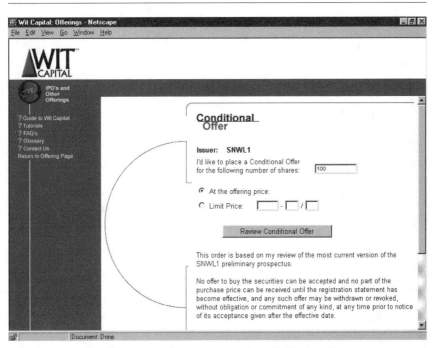

Source: Courtesy of Wit Capital (www.witcapital.com). Used with permission.

reports. "Research" is probably one of the best sections in the Wit Capital Web site. We highly recommend that investors use this section to get insight into many of the publicly traded Internet companies.

"Market Insight" provides investors with tutorials and educational resources. Here you can view both the NASDAQ and NYSE stock index. There is also valuable IPO news from other IPO data Web site providers (see Figure 7.13 on page 128).

"Customer Care" links beginners to tutorials, and to question and answer pages.

Wit Capital has plans to build an after-hours trading facility that will allow investors to trade securities after the major markets close on Wall Street. Although not in effect at the time of this publishing, we think this will be of major interest to investors in the future.

Figure 7.9   Conditional Offer Verification Page

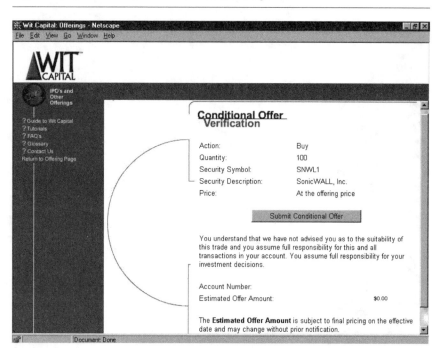

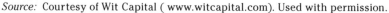

Source: Courtesy of Wit Capital (www.witcapital.com). Used with permission.

For future reference, Wit Capital maintains a section of the Web site where you can view previous offerings they have distributed online. To give you an idea of the type of offerings and the number of shares Wit Capital typically underwrites, let's look at Table 7.1 on page 129 showing the underwriting recap as of May 1999. (These figures were taken from the Wit Capital prospectus, dated May 1999.)

Although the numbers seem to represent a small percentage of the total underwriting, Wit Capital provides the best opportunity for individual investors to obtain initial shares in upcoming IPOs. As Wit Capital's membership grows, they anticipate being able to participate in a larger number of IPOs and also to have a larger number of shares to allocate to their investors. This will provide a

Figure 7.10   Conditional Offer Acknowledgment Page

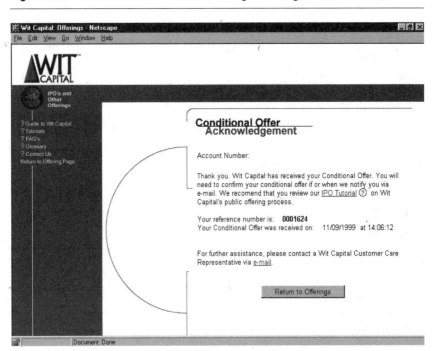

Source: Courtesy of Wit Capital (www.witcapital.com). Used with permission.

growing opportunity for individuals to get a piece of the action at Wit Capital.

Wit Capital also is the best place to open an online brokerage account for IPO investing, due to their reputable and highly regarded management team and leadership. Most importantly, Wit Capital had an excellent track record with IPOs in 1999. They participated in many of the sweetheart deals of the year, including CBS Marketwatch, VerticalNet, Healtheon (WebMD), iVillage, Cobalt Networks, and FREEMARKETS.

One of the most important key factors in investing with Wit Capital has been the flipping penalty. Initial shares that are allocated to you as an investor must be held for at least 60 days following the offering or you will probably not be allocated shares in any

Figure 7.11 Manage My Account Page

Source: Courtesy of Wit Capital (www.witcapital.com). Used with permission.

other new issues until the 60 days are up. Many times we had to wait roughly 60 days until we had the chance or the opportunity to again be allocated shares. On occasion, however, we were allocated shares in accounts even after we had flipped.

Friedman, Billings, Ramsey & Co., Inc.
http://www.fbr.com

Friedman, Billings, Ramsey & Co., Inc. (FBR) has an affiliate on-line broker-dealer called fbr.com (See Figure 7.14 on page 130). fbr.com states in their Web site that FBR "will make up to 50 percent of the shares which FBR receives in an offering available to online investors."[1] Although fbr.com is a fairly new Web site—launched in April 1999—with services available to the individual investor, we believe that their aggressive marketing will make them a contender in

Figure 7.12   Stock Order Entry Page

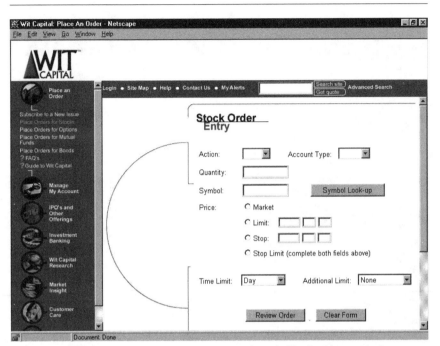

Source: Courtesy of Wit Capital (www.witcapital.com). Used with permission.

the battle of supplying IPOs to the retail investor. Our first dealings with fbr.com involved their very first online offering, Career-builder.com, in the beginning of May 1999. Unlike Wit Capital, fbr.com states that they do not penalize you for flipping shares. We are testing this claim for our readers and will report our findings on www.IPOguys.com. As such, we flipped (sold) 200 shares of Career-builder.com 10 minutes after the stock started trading. Although we do not condone flipping, sometimes it is recommended. One of us bought 200 shares @ $13.00 a share on May 11, 1999, and sold 200 shares @ $17.75 on May 12, 1999, achieving a nice profit of $950 in less than 10 minutes.

The process to open an account is very similar to that of Wit Capital: (1) apply online, (2) print out the application and sign, and (3) mail in the application with initial deposit of $2,000.

Figure 7.13   Welcome to Market Insight Page

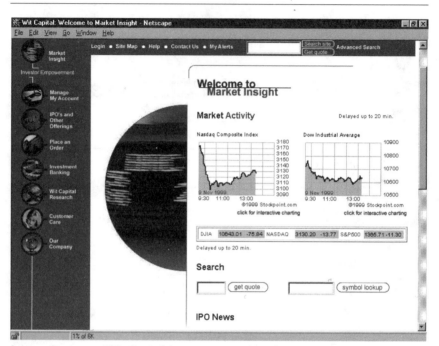

Source: Courtesy of Wit Capital (www.witcapital.com). Used with permission.

fbr.com's Web site has three main sections, "Offering Marketplace," Online Trading, and Research Desktop. "Offering Marketplace" lists upcoming offerings on which investors can place a conditional to buy. Placing a conditional offer at fbr.com is very easy:

Step 1: Before Placing a Conditional Offer: Educate Yourself. If you are considering an investment in an offering, educate yourself about the company making the offering by reading the preliminary prospectus found as a link to each offering's posting on this site. It is your guide to understanding their company's business and management team, as well as the risks involved in the investment. We will also post on the site the "Open" period, the time within which you can submit a Conditional Offer (C.O.).

Table 7.1   Wit Capital's Underwriting Recap

IPO	Major Underwriter	Date	# of Shares Underwritten	% of Total Shares Underwritten
Marketwatch.com	BT. Alexander Brown	1/15/99	69,000	2
Verticalnet.com	Lehman Brothers	2/10/99	70,000	2
Prodigy	Bear Stearns & Co.	2/10/99	184,000	2
MiningCo.com	Bear Stearns & Co. BT. Alexander Brown	3/23/99	69,000	2
OneMain.com	& Hambrecht & Quist BT. Alexander Brown	3/24/99	402,500	4
iTurf	& Hambrecht & Quist BancBoston	4/8/99	75,000	2
NetPerceptions	Robertson Stephens	4/22/99	125,000	3
Mpath Interactive	BancBoston Robertson Stephens	4/28/99	125,000	3

Source: Courtesy of Wit Capital (www.witcapital.com). Used with permission.

Step 2: "Open" Period, 2 to 3 Days Before Expected Pricing. Place a C.O. At this time, the period for placing a C.O. is open. You will need to do the following: login to the secured part of the site, download and review the preliminary prospectus of the offering you are interested in and complete a few offering-related questions. Now you're ready to place a C.O. Enter the number of shares you want to purchase and your "Limit Price Range," the range in which you are willing to purchase the stock. If the final stock price falls below or above your specified range, your order will be ineligible for the offering. Your Limit Price Range may be equal to or must fall within the expected price range for the offering specified in the preliminary prospectus. (Example: Expected price range: $13 to $16; your limit price range: $13 to $15; offering final price: $16; your C.O. deemed ineligible.) Note: At any time during the open period, you may modify or cancel an existing C.O.

Figure 7.14   fbr.com Home Page

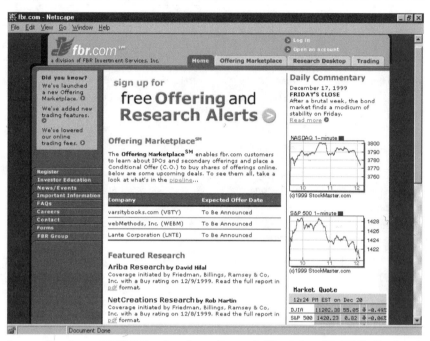

Source: Courtesy of FBR & Co., Inc. (www.fbr.com) (December 17, 1999). Used with permission.

Step 3: Expected Pricing Date: Pricing.   Before an offering begins trading, the registration statement for the offering must be declared effective by the SEC. This typically occurs the day before the offering is expected to trade, but occasionally occurs the morning of trading. After the final price has been set and the offering has been declared effective, you will be notified via e-mail of the price and will have a final opportunity to cancel your C.O.

Step 4: Selection and Allocation.   Unless you cancel your C.O., it will be entered into our computer-generated random selection process. You will then receive an e-mail alert that you did, or did not, receive an allocation of shares in the

Figure 7.15 fbr.com Updates

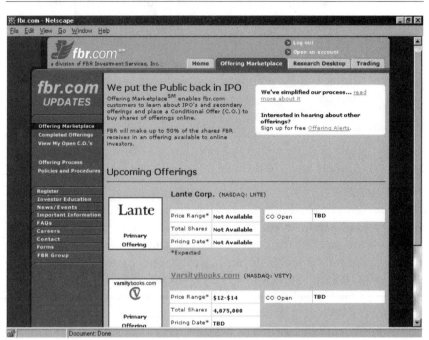

Source: Courtesy of FBR & Co., Inc. (www.fbr.com) (December 17, 1999). Used with permission.

offering. If you are allocated shares, fbr.com will accept your C.O. and a binding contract is formed. The allocated shares will appear in your online trading account before the security begins to trade in the secondary market. Congratulations! You now own shares in a public offering.[2]

There is a new buzz in the IPO market and it is fbr.com's Offering Marketplace (see Figure 7.15). The IPOguys spoke with fbr.com. Discussion primarily centered on their new "Offering Marketplace" and the potentital impact on individual investors:

What is this Offering Marketplace thing anyway? Through their "Offering Marketplace," fbr.com has developed a proprietary IPO distribution system that enables them to distribute IPO shares to a large number of investors.

Why is this important? Listen up shrewd IPO investor . . . this could mean lots of IPO shares for you in the near future. By improving upon the traditional IPO allocation system, fbr.com now claims that they can distribute up to 100 percent of shares to individual investors if they so choose. This was physically impossible in the past under traditional distribution limitations. The traditional distribution is more like 80 percent institutional investors, 20 percent individual investors.

Traditional limitations. Under the old distribution system— conditional offers were placed, the deal was priced, and only then (after the pricing) could conditional offers be allocated. fbr.com estimated that the greatest number of online investor participants could participate prior to Offering Marketplace was under 5,000. Under the new "Offering Marketplace" system, fbr.com said they can process the entire offering in hyper-speed potentially allowing millions of investors to participate. From 600,000 to 10,000,000 shares distribution in one shot . . . now that is definitely the logistical efficiency improvement of the year thus far.

Why Offering Marketplace is a better system. Offering Marketplace does not always require this reconfirmation process of conditional offers. They are able to allocate millions of shares within a very short period of time (minutes or seconds).

The end of the syndicate. Since online banks will now have the capability to underwrite and distribute an entire deal to their individual clients via the Web, does this spell the end of the syndicate? Maybe so, but probably not completely. Underwriters are still most likely going to want to spread out their risk on certain deals . . . so there is a good chance that multiple underwriters will be involved.

However, the number of syndicate members may decrease over the long term.

Impact on institutional investors. How do institutional investors feel about greater and greater percentages of IPO allocations going into the hands of individual investors? It certainly is a balancing act for any underwriter to satisfy the tremendous demand for everyone who wants access to IPO shares. But fbr.com is confident they will be able to deliver the product since they would be able to underwrite an entire deal by themselves if they wanted to.

Impact on capital formation process and IPO investing arena. This is just one more nail in the coffin of the traditional capital formation process. The potential impact is enormous. We see development as nothing less than the continuation of the trend that is helping shift some of the wealth from the hands of the extremely wealthy into the hands of the prepared individual investor.

Impact on fbr.com. fbr.com believes that issuing companies will be drawn to them to underwrite their deals because fbr.com can distribute to a broad audience of investors, which should improve the stability of the stock over both the short and long term. The simple fact that IPO shares will be placed in the hands of individuals who actually want to own them, rather than have shares placed in the hands of clients who are simply out to flip the shares on the first day or two of trading. fbr.com believes their "Offering Marketplace" model is not only in the best interest of the company . . . but also in the best interest of the individual investors and their institutional clients.

We salute fbr.com for their recent steps to put a distribution system in place that allows more shares for the individual investor. We hope that their new distribution model does mean more IPO shares for individual investors. Time will tell, but the potential is huge for the individual investor and warrants extra attention.

The Online Trading section at fbr.com has many links including, market data, quotes, charts, new headlines, and mutual funds. Like the other online firms at fbr.com, you can buy and sell stocks and mutual funds. The Research Desktop is probably one of the most valuable tools for the individual investor. Account holders at fbr.com can get access to FBR's high quality institutional investment reports. fbr.com is an affiliate of FBR, which represents a great opportunity for the individual investor to have access to these research reports.

FBR & Co. is not new to the underwriting industry, and we believe the fbr.com Web site and service will be a great opportunity for the individual investor. The first two IPOs distributed online to individual investors through the fbr.com Web site were Careerbuilder.com and CAIS Internet. The most recent, and noteworthy IPO that was underwritten by FBR was Red Hat, the company responsible for the Linux "open-source" operating system. fbr.com maintains a section of the Web site where you can view previous offerings they have distributed online. We would like to note that at the time of our submission of the manuscript to our publisher we received allocations in ASD Systems and NetCreations.

WR Hambrecht + Co.
http://www.wrhambrecht.com
http://www.openipo.com

WR Hambrecht + Co. provides investors the opportunity to buy IPOs through both a traditional format and an "auction" style format called "OpenIPO" (see Figure 7.16). The OpenIPO method is interesting and is gaining ground although it does not seem to create the same "edge" or advantage for investors in the short term that traditional IPOs have in the past. WR Hambrecht + Co. believes their edge is that all investors—individuals and institutions—are on equal footing in the IPO process. All bids have the same weight and depend on price, not number of shares. Compared with other online investment banks, the OpenIPO model provides individual investors the best opportunity to purchase shares in upcoming initial public offerings.

The OpenIPO format to purchase initial shares takes place in an online auction. Investors place bids at the price they are willing to pay for "x" number of shares, 100 shares minimum bids. Bids can

Figure 7.16   WR Hambrecht + Co. Home Page

Source: Courtesy of WR Hambrecht + Co. (www.wrhambrecht.com). Used with permission.

be more or less than the suggested "price range." Bids are the same as an "indication of interest." The auction closes when the SEC declares the offering effective. The auction engine counts down from highest bid price to the price at which all shares in the offering are filled. The winning bids all pay the same price, the offering price. Investors who bid above that price receive all the shares they wanted, investors who bid less than offering price receive no shares, and those investors who bid at the offering receive a pro rata amount of shares. Shares are purchased through a traditional online brokerage account at WR Hambrecht + Co. (see Figure 7.17).

The conditional offer or bid is similar to the other online brokerage firms in that once you place your bid, you can always change or cancel right up to the offering date. Unlike other auction

Figure 7.17   WR Hambrecht + Co. Offerings

Source: Courtesy of WR Hambrecht + Co. (www.wrhambrecht.com). Used with permission.

formats, your bid or conditional offer is kept private and confidential, no other members will see your bid price.

The idea behind the auction format is that the market sets the offering price, not investment bankers. Instead of the large institutions and favored investment banking clients getting the majority of the initial shares, individual investors have the same chance and opportunity to buy the initial shares. The auction format places everyone on an equal standing.

One of the great strengths of the OpenIPO method and auction format is that the entire allotment of shares is sold through the auction. No other shares are available to the public. OpenIPO has instituted the most democratic form of distribution of initial shares in the industry today. The concept is revolutionary; whether it works remains to be seen. For now, we resolve to simply keep an eye on WR Hambrecht + Co.

The company also participates in traditional initial public offerings other than OpenIPO offerings. These traditional offerings are similar to those made by Wit Capital, and fbr.com. Offerings are posted on the traditional "deals" link. Investors who want to place "conditional offers" can call the trade desk to place offers. Currently, you can't place offers online. We recently opened an account with WR Hambrecht + Co. Here are some e-mail interview questions we asked them about their new online investment bank.

IPOguys: Do you think the "Dutch Auction" business model will work for selling initial public offerings? If so, why will it work?

Bill Hambrecht: Yes. Two deals completed (Ravenswood and Salon.com), the third, Andover.net, currently is in registration and should be completed next week. We are the only investment bank with a fair way of pricing and allocation of IPOs. Other investment banks merely distribute traditional offerings via online accounts. The pricing is still done by investment bankers.

IPOguys: What Public Relations steps has WR Hambrecht + Co. taken to inform individual investors about the opportunity available to buy initial public offerings online?

Sharon Smith: We have not had to do any paid advertising but have had several articles in *The Wall Street Journal, Fortune, Forbes, Upside* magazine, *The New York Times,* and so on. (several articles are available on our Web site). We are trying to educate the media as well as the investment community as to what is a "successful" IPO. The purpose of an initial public offering is to get the issuing company as much money as possible; when a deal is priced at $15 and the first trade is at $90, the company gets $15 and the favored clients and institutions get $90. The investors who really want to own the stock end up buying at an inflated price.

IPOguys: How many offerings has the "OpenIPO" side model completed this year?

WR Hambrecht + Co.:   Two, third in process.

IPOguys: The IPOguys believe the investment banking industry as a whole has not done a good job in educating individual investors about the "new opportunity" in buying IPOs online. How does WR Hambrecht + Co plan on providing a "knowledge base" for its clients, thus empowering them to become more educated investors in regards to IPO investing?

WR Hambrecht + Co.:   We are constantly, through the media and talking to clients, trying to educate the investment community and the media.[3]

WR Hambrecht + Co. is a full-service online investment bank including online brokerage, trading, mergers and acquisitions advisory services, research, and a private investments area providing accredited investors the opportunity to invest alongside WR Hambrecht + Co in venture investments where WRH+Co acts as a principal (no other investment bank is doing this).

E*TRADE
http://www.etrade.com

E*TRADE is a highly publicized online brokerage firm, and therefore one of the names people are familiar with. Because E*TRADE now has over one million accounts, obtaining IPO shares is very competitive. They state in their Q&A section that all initial shares are allocated to members at the best of their ability. Similar to most other online brokerage firms, E*TRADE tries to allocate at least 100 shares to members in good standing who place indications of interest during the specified time.

E*TRADE has a section on investing in IPOs called the IPO Center. The IPO customer bulletin places all conditional offers inquiries for IPOs on this page. Once the offering is posted on the bulletin, members generally have between 30 minutes and a couple of hours to place an indication of interest.

Once the offering for shares in the IPO is posted, investors are required to fill out an investor profile form online. The form has about 10 to 15 questions regarding the investor's investing history and is used as a prequalification to purchasing IPOs. Once you have filled out this form and submitted it to E*TRADE, they will let you know immediately if you have qualified to place an indication of interest for the IPO. E*TRADE also requires you to acknowledge that you have read the prospectus prior to placing an indication of interest. Once you place an indication of interest, it is considered firm and you are not required to reconfirm your offer.

The IPO will generally be priced in the evening, and investors will be notified via their "Account Alert" inbox whether they have been allocated shares in the new offering. Investors must have the funds in their account to pay for at least 100 shares as a prerequisite to being allocated shares in any offering. (Similar to the other previously mentioned online brokerage firms, E*TRADE maintains a section of the Web site where you can view previous offerings they have distributed online.) E*TRADE also provides investors an online brokerage department where individuals can buy and sell stocks, bonds, and mutual funds.

E*OFFERING
http://www.eoffering.com

In January 1999, E*OFFERING, the Internet investment bank funded in part by E*TRADE Group, Inc., and Sandy Robertson, founder and former CEO of Robertson Stephens & Co., was founded. It provides full-service investment research and capital markets capabilities to institutional and individual investors (see Figure 7.18). This move should provide greater focus on E*TRADE's investment banking activities, which can only help improve the quantity and quality of the IPOs E*TRADE is able to offer.

Once you have opened your E*TRADE account, you must register at www.eoffering.com to receive E*TRADE's improved IPO services through E*OFFERING:

- Immediate e-mail notification of E*OFFERING's public offerings when they become available.

- E-mail alerts of timely market insights and new research that E*OFFERING's analysts have posted.

- E-mail alerts that signal when critical steps in the IPO process for E*OFFERING's companies have been completed.

In addition to these improved Internet e-mail alert features, E*OFFERING states that it will offer "up to 50 percent of every IPO

Figure 7.18   E*OFFERING Home Page

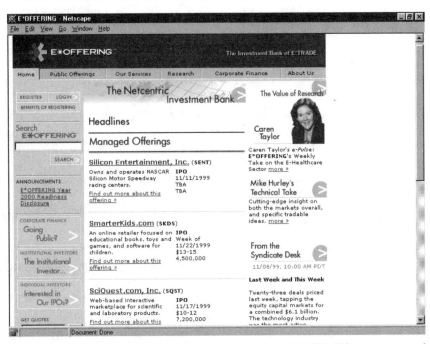

Source: Courtesy of E*OFFERING (www.eoffering.com). E*OFFERING is a registered trademark. All rights reserved. Used with permission.

or secondary offering it manages to E*TRADE customers. As such, E*OFFERING should continue to be one of the top players in the battle for offering IPOs to the individual investor (see Figure 7.19).

We bought our first IPO shares in one of E*OFFERING's deals recently. On September 23, 1999, we bought 100 shares of Cybergold, Inc. We sold it later on the first day of trading for $9.87 a share. It wasn't the greatest gain in the world, but we didn't lose money either. This has been the only IPO we have been allocated by E*OFFERING this year.

The success the individual investor will be able to achieve purchasing IPOs through E*TRADE and E*OFFERING remains to be seen. On the downside, the large number of accounts competing for shares could potentially make it difficult for the individual investor

Figure 7.19 Public Offering Page

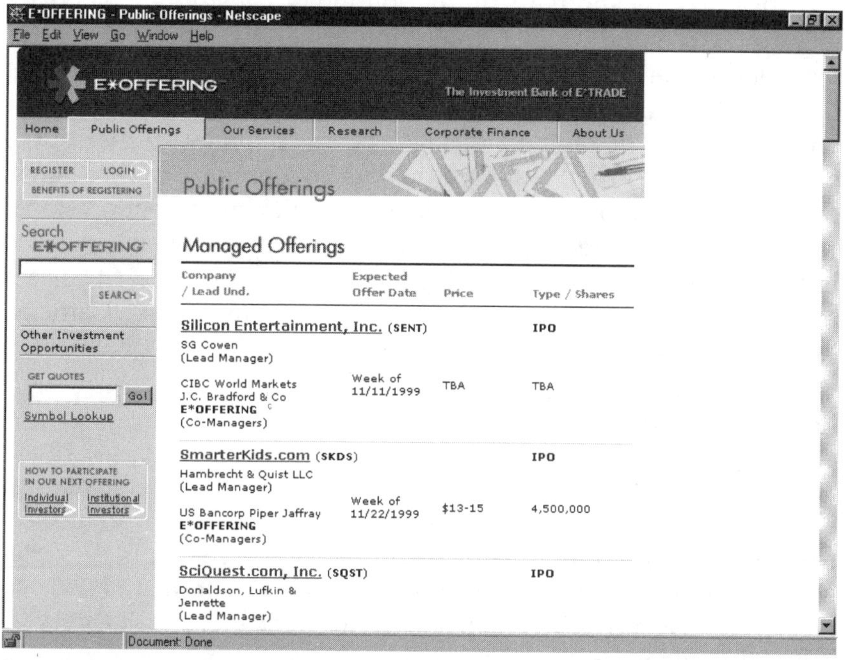

to receive any allocation. Shares are generally randomly allocated among interested customers after a review of the applicants' holding records in prior public offerings, and subject to priority allocation for Power E*TRADE Platinum customers. Accounts with a history of short holding periods receive a lesser allocation priority in offerings where demand for shares exceeds the supply available for distribution.[4]

On the upside, E*TRADE should be able to leverage its size (i.e., the number of accounts) to increase the number of deals it is involved in, and to increase the number of shares they are allocated in each deal. More shares in more deals, of course, should mean more shares for the individual investor. The question is, will the increase in shares outpace the increase in new accounts demanding IPOs?

Donaldson, Lufkin & Jenrette Company
http://www.dljdirect.com

DLJdirect is another firm that provides investors the opportunity to purchase IPOs at the offering price. A major obstacle for most individual investors is the $100,000 minimum deposit that DLJdirect requires as a prequalification to participating in the purchase of IPOs. The online offering process is similar to that of the other brokerage firms, although there is no mention of a first-come, first-serve allocation process. In fact, their allocation section states that clients with larger accounts and also those who have a "track record" with their company will get priority over others. DLJdirect also provides investors the opportunity to buy and sell stocks, bonds, and mutual funds online.

Charles Schwab
http://www.schwab.com

Schwab.com is similar to DLJdirect.com in that individuals with accounts of $100,000 or more are generally the investors that have the opportunity to purchase IPOs. Schwab states that only their Signature Platinum accounts (those with at least $50,000 and $1,000,000 or more in assets) will be considered for allocations of IPOs. However, the feedback we have received from investors who have $50,000 or larger accounts is that it is difficult to receive any IPO allocations. The following Web site, http://www.schwab-ipos.com, shows upcoming offerings. Schwab also provides investors with online trading of stocks, bonds, and mutual funds.

The latest news from Schwab is that they are combining forces with three venture capital firms and two other online brokerage firms to form the largest group of online trading accounts in the United States. The strategic goal of these relationships is to provide their clients improved access to IPOs at the offering price. We discuss this new endeavor for Charles Schwab & Co. in Chapter 9.

E InvestmentBank (Wedbush Morgan Securities)
http://www.einvestmentbank.com

E InvestmentBank provides investors direct access to public offerings and private placements underwritten or managed by Wedbush Morgan Securities. We found it very easy to apply online, and the Web site is user-friendly as well (see Figures 7.20 and 7.21). The individual investor can be up and running with this firm on completion of an online account application and approval. As their Web site states, "If you have a temporary or activated account with us you can subscribe to offerings immediately."[5] Investors need to deposit a minimum of $2,000 to open an account.

E InvestmentBank provides each client with an "E Order Book" where account holders go to manage their conditional offers. IPOs are distributed, or allocated, on a first-come, first-serve basis, in 100-share increments. Once 100 shares have been allocated, they will allocate the next round of 100 shares through the list in the same order in which the first round of 100 shares were offered. E InvestmentBank asks that their clients hold IPOs after pricing for at least 60 days, but does not restrict them in any way from selling shares at

Figure 7.20   E InvestmentBank Home Page

Source: Courtesy of E InvestmentBank (www.einvestmentbank.com). Used with permission.

Figure 7.21 E InvestmentBank Alerts

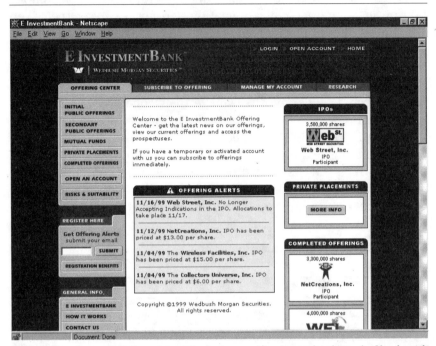

Source: Courtesy of E InvestmentBank (www.einvestmentbank.com). Used with permission.

any time. However, similar to Wit Capital and E*Trade, clients (flippers) who sell shares prior to the suggested holding period may be excluded from future offerings.

E InvestmentBank also posts free online research reports that you can view at any time on their Web site. These reports mostly involve companies where Wedbush Morgan Securities was part of the underwriting deal, although this may not be exclusively the case.

The number and quality of IPOs that E InvestmentBank is offering their online investors has been improving, which leads us to believe that E InvestmentBank will be a major player in the battle to provide individual investors with quality IPOs. At the time of the writing of this book, we have both opened accounts and started placing indications of interest at E InvestmentBank. On November 5, 1999, one of us received an allocation of 50 shares in "Wireless

Facilities, Inc." (WFII) at $15.00 a share. This was our first alloca-
tion at E InvestmentBank.

IPO Syndicate (Mercer Partners, Inc.)
http://www.iposyndicate.com

Mercer Partners, Inc. recently announced their entry into the
market of offering IPOs to the retail investor online with the launch
of IPOSyndicate.com. The IPOSyndicate.com Web site states that
they are focused on small cap, high-growth companies, and con-
cisely summarizes their mission. "IPOSyndicate.com is the next
generation Internet-based financial mall targeting the individual investor. We are a comprehensive financial community and a portal
for both investors and issuers of equity securities. Inside you will
find a forum for online investing, news, and research complete with
navigational tools that facilitate the trading process through our
own proprietary products and software. We offer Initial Public Offerings, Secondary & Follow-on Offerings, Private Equity Investments, Research, Online Investing in stocks and mutual funds, and
Day Trading."[6]

Investors can open an account online very quickly, most likely
in under 30 minutes. The minimum initial deposit to open an account is $2,000. Investors are then provided an "Indication Book"
where they can place and manage their indications of interest. Like
many of the companies we have previously discussed, IPOSyndicate
allocates shares on a first-come, first-serve basis.

The IPOSyndicate Web site has an area where you can obtain
recent market news and information. Of special interest to the day
traders, IPOSyndicate also has an area totally dedicated to "Day
Trading" that contains proprietary software and services for purchase or lease.

Summary

- Online investment banks provide the greatest opportunity
  for the IPO investor to obtain IPO shares.
- The current online investment banks offering shares to the
  individual investor include:

Wit Capital.

E*TRADE.

E*OFFERING.

Friedman, Billings, Ramsey & Co. (FBR.com).

WR Hambrecht + Co.

Donaldson, Lufkin & Jenrette Company.

Charles Schwab & Co.

Mercer Partners, Inc. (IPO Syndicate).

Wedbush Morgan Securities (E InvestmentBank).

- We found that we could most easily do business with and obtain IPOs from Wit Capital, FBR, and E InvestmentBank. If you are looking for a fast start in the IPO arena, we suggest opening an account at Wit Capital first, and FBR.com second, followed by E InvestmentBank. We also highly recommend the other online investment banks mentioned in this chapter; however, they all provide great promise for the IPO investor looking to obtain allocations of IPOs at the offering price.

chapter 8

secrets, software, and technology

staying ahead of the game

Many tools are available to individual investors to help them succeed in the area of IPO investing. In this chapter, we describe our personal favorites.

Monitoring and Notification Software

This tool is our number one favorite IPO investing tool. The hardest part about getting in on an IPO is placing your conditional offer in a timely enough manner to result in allocation of those shares. This software helps the individual investor with that task.

When an online investment bank has IPOs to offer to their online accounts, they typically post the IPO availability on a specific page at their Web site. It is the individual investor's responsibility to monitor these pages and place an order prior to the cutoff time. Web monitoring and notification software watches these specific pages and notifies the user when changes occur.

E*TRADE posts availability on a Web page called their IPO Bulletin. Wit Capital calls it their "Current Offerings." These two sites, in addition to many of the others listed previously, have a limited time frame in which you can place your orders for IPOs. With E*TRADE, the window you have to place your order to buy can be less than an hour. Wit Capital's window is usually a standard 11:59 A.M. cutoff for morning postings, and 11:59 P.M. cutoff for IPOs posted in the afternoon or evening.

Early on, when Wit Capital distributed shares completely on a first-come, first-served basis, this tool was absolutely critical. If you were able to pick up a Web page change quickly enough to beat the mad rush to place orders, chances are you would receive allocation.

Wit Capital's present allocation rules and procedures allow the individual investor an 8- to 12-hour window to place an order, but we have still found this software extremely useful in making sure you receive notification and place your order before the cutoff. (Note: We no longer use this software to monitor Wit Capital.)

NetLookout by Frugalsoft
http://www.frugalsoft.com

NetLookout is our preferred monitoring and notification software. When we first came across NetLookout, it was an excellent monitoring tool that was capable of monitoring Web pages every two minutes and notifying the user with a message box on the screen and/or a tone or wave file. It did, however, lack the capability of e-mail notification of the Web site change. On request, the developer has since added e-mail notification and has also increased the monitoring frequency to check for Web page changes once every minute. The developer was also very responsive to bug fixes and enhancement suggestions. This software was also the easiest to set up and the most user friendly. The NetLookout software is currently $20.00 retail.

E-Mail Programs

E-mail programs are extremely helpful in successful IPO investing.

Eudora Pro
http://www.eudora.com

Eudora Pro is our top pick for e-mail programs. Eudora has e-mail filters, which allow you to search for key words in the e-mail including sender and subject, and will even scan the body of the message. You can have e-mails that meet a specified criteria forwarded to your pager/cell phone, and even autorespond to the sender. This is the only e-mail package we found that allows you to automatically respond during the conditional offer reaffirmation process when you need to confirm your conditional offer. There are some other e-mail management software packages that allow you to properly confirm your conditional offer; however, we found them very difficult to set up and lacking severely in user friendliness.

Microsoft Outlook Express

Many of today's computers come standard with the Windows operating system and this e-mail package. Like Eudora, Microsoft Outlook Express has good e-mail filtering capability and will allow you to filter e-mails based on sender, subject, text body, and other criteria. Microsoft Outlook Express also has autoforwarding capabilities, allowing you to send e-mails to your pager or cell phone for timely notification.

We have been informed that the autoreply portion of Microsoft Outlook Express does allow the user to automatically respond to e-mails in the reaffirmation process required by some online banks. An alternative is to use a text pager that allows you to reply to e-mails. Have your e-mails from the online brokerage firms sent to your text pager where you can confirm right from the pager. Otherwise, you will have to get to a computer to complete the reaffirmation process once you receive a forwarded message.

Wireless Internet Access

Always seem to be away from your computer? One solution is to go with wireless Internet access.

Palm Pilot and the Minstrel Modem

We bought the Palm Pilot Professional and the Wireless Minstrel modem to provide mobile Internet access and e-mail capabilities. At the time of this writing, the Minstrel modem and Palm Pilot Professional can be purchased for around $700.00 retail for both. You can access every online brokerage firm's Web pages and your accounts through the wireless system. When you download the Web browser for your palm pilot, we recommend using Proxiweb (http://www.proxiweb.com). Proxiweb is the only handheld browser that we were able to find that supports SSL, and Java Scripting found on both Wit Capital's and E*TRADE's Web site. We tried many other compact wireless devices, but most of them ran on Windows CE bundled with Pocket Explorer which at the time of this writing could not access the level of security required by Wit Capital and E*TRADE. A good Web site to monitor the newest in Windows CE technology is Chris De Herrera's Windows CE Web site (http://www.cewindows.net/).

Laptop Computer

If being compact is not an issue, you can simply buy a wireless modem for your laptop computer. Only a few wireless modems are available for the laptop PC, but we were able to locate two. The first one we found is the Sierra Wireless AirCard 300 (http://www.sierrawireless.com). Another wireless modem for the laptop PC we found is called the Ricochet Wireless Modem (http://www.ricochet.net).

Multiple Accounts

When opening accounts at the various online investment banks, we started out by opening one account. We then realized that the rule of thumb is that investors generally get only 100 shares, sometimes 200 at the most. We then decided to open more accounts. Legally, you can have one account in your name, one account in your spouse's name, and one joint account for husband and wife. If you're married, this can be a good way to accumulate large numbers of shares. Another idea is to have an account in the name of your legally registered sole proprietorship, business, or corporation. Readers should verify the rules of each online investment bank for opening up more than one account.

Opening multiple accounts with the same online investment bank allowed us to get from 300 to 600 shares total. We only suggest this method as a way to increase your chances of getting allocated shares, remembering that it is important to be selective in your choice of IPOs. Once you have multiple accounts at several online investment banks that offer IPOs, you may find that at times you are able to obtain more shares than you can afford. On many occasions, we have passed on allocations in IPOs that were not in our "absolutely-positively-need-to-buy" list.

IPOguys Web Site
http://www.ipoguys.com

Find links to all the online investment banks that are offering access to IPOs.

Sign up for our *free* IPO Journal at www.ipoguys.com and receive:

- The latest news and trends that will impact IPO investing and the online investing community as a whole.
- The latest interviews from leaders in the IPO investing arena, from online investment banks to IPO Web site owners to online individual investors.
- Tips and tricks from real IPO investors.
- Rankings and research of the online investment banking industry. What online investment banks are allocating the most shares to individual investors?

This information and more can be found at the IPOguys Web site. We are dedicated to providing the online individual IPO investor with the highest quality information. Don't expect to be bombarded with e-mails of little or no value. We send out e-mails only when there is news of significant value to the online individual IPO investor.

Stay in touch with us at http://www.ipoguys.com to ensure your success in the IPO investing arena.

Summary

- Many tools are available to help the individual investor. The two most important tools that should be in your arsenal are

Web site monitoring and e-mail pager (text messaging) notification.

- Wireless Internet access makes the IPO investor more efficient and more flexible by providing freedom and mobility away from a desktop workstation.

- Staying ahead of the game is 99 percent of the battle. Find out about new companies offering IPOs before everyone else. You can also subscribe to our free IPO Journal report (http://www.ipoguys.com).

chapter 9

ipos and the future for online individual investors

We want to end this book by talking a little about the future. As you begin investing, it is easy to get lost in the loads of available information and to lose sight of the big picture. When we say "big picture," we mean the major changes taking place in the financial and investing communities as a result of the Internet. Although it is important to pay attention to detail when making IPO investing decisions, don't lose sight of the revolution that surrounds you every day. Staying mindful of that big picture will allow you to recognize and capitalize on the newest investment opportunities as they become available.

We can only speculate what future changes will have (big picture) ramifications and open new doors to profits for the individual investor (see Table 9.1). The speed of change in Internet time makes the future that much more uncertain, and commentary on the future that much more difficult. Nevertheless, we will take our best stab at identifying the top developments in the financial and investing communities that will ultimately lead to new opportunities.

We have combined our research with the opinions of everyone we interviewed for this book to provide some insight into the

Table 9.1 1999 YTD IPO Performance (Detail)

Offering Date	Company Name	SYMB	Offering Price ($)	12/6/99 Price ($)	Change (%)
11/17/99	AGILENT TECHNOLOGIES INC	A	30	46.13	54
03/26/99	AUTOBYTEL.COM INC (AUTO BY TEL CORP)	ABTL	23	15.00	-35
04/16/99	ACCREDO HEALTH INC	ACDO	16	28.00	75
09/29/99	ACME COMMUNICATIONS INC	ACME	23	36.50	59
07/29/99	ACCRUE SOFTWARE INC	ACRU	10	56.25	463
07/15/99	AUDIBLE INC	ADBL	9	13.31	48
05/07/99	ADFORCE INC (IMGIS INC)	ADFC	15	43.50	190
10/20/99	AETHER SYSTEMS INC	AETH	16	74.38	365
08/12/99	US AGGREGATES INC	AGA	15	11.50	-23
08/19/99	AGILE SOFTWARE CORP	AGIL	21	146.88	599
09/30/99	AMERICAN HOME MORTGAGE HOLDINGS INC	AHMH	6	6.75	13
07/29/99	AIRONET WIRELESS COMMUNICATIONS INC	AIRO	11	61.38	458
10/29/99	AKAMAI TECHNOLOGIES INC	AKAM	26	214.44	725
07/01/99	ALASKA PACIFIC BANCSHARES INC	AKPB	10	10.50	5
03/11/99	COMMUNITY CAPITAL BANCSHARES INC	ALBY	10	11.00	10
01/22/99	ALLAIRE CORP	ALLR	20	174.00	770
05/14/99	ALLOY ONLINE INC	ALOY	15	19.63	31
11/17/99	ALASKA COMMUNICATIONS SYSTEMS GROUP INC (ALEC HOLDINGS INC)	ALSK	14	13.63	-3
11/30/99	AMERICAN FINANCIAL HOLDING CORP INC	AMFH	10	12.06	21
02/04/99	ALBANY MOLECULAR RESEARCH INC	AMRI	20	28.00	40
02/11/99	AMERICAN NATIONAL FINANCIAL INC	ANFI	6	3.94	-34
03/04/99	ANTENNA TV SA	ANTV	15	14.75	-2
07/15/99	ANYTHING INTERNET CORP	ANYI	6	2.50	-58
05/20/99	@PLAN.INC (AT PLAN INC)	APLN	14	12.78	-9
06/18/99	APPNET SYSTEMS INC	APNT	12	57.13	376
06/22/99	ARIBA INC	ARBA	23	216.63	842
10/28/99	ALLIED RISER COMMUNICATIONS CORP	ARCC	18	20.56	14
04/22/99	AREMISSOFT CORP	AREM	5	23.06	361
03/08/99	ARGOSY EDUCATION GROUP INC	ARGY	14	4.50	-68
08/16/99	ALLIANCE RESOURCE PARTNERS LP	ARLP	19	13.38	-30
07/21/99	ART TECHNOLOGY GROUP INC	ARTG	12	75.00	525
11/10/99	ASD SYSTEMS INC	ASDS	8	20.88	161

Table 9.1 *Continued*

Offering Date	Company Name	SYMB	Offering Price ($)	12/6/99 Price ($)	Change (%)
09/22/99	ASHFORD.COM INC (NEWWATCH CO)	ASFD	13	18.13	39
07/01/99	ASK JEEVES INC (ASKJEEVES.COM)	ASKJ	14	129.00	821
08/12/99	ACTIVE SOFTWARE INC	ASWX	11	72.25	557
10/04/99	ALTIGEN COMMUNICATIONS INC	ATGN	10	12.44	24
04/30/99	APPLIED THEORY CORP	ATHY	16	20.75	30
09/23/99	ALTEON WEBSYSTEMS INC	ATON	19	111.25	486
05/27/99	AUDIOCODES	AUDC	14	67.13	379
03/22/99	AUTOWEB.COM INC	AWEB	14	11.44	−18
01/28/99	AMERICAN AXLE & MANUFACTURING HOLDINGS INC	AXL	17	12.25	−28
06/09/99	AZURIX CORP	AZX	19	7.38	−61
08/25/99	BAMBOO.COM INC	BAMB	7	13.69	96
08/10/99	BLOCKBUSTER INC	BBI	15	15.13	1
09/21/99	BROADBASE SOFTWARE INC	BBSW	14	85.75	513
07/20/99	BE INC	BEOS	6	13.69	128
07/09/99	BETA OIL & GAS INC	BETA	6	7.69	28
11/02/99	BE FREE INC	BFRE	12	52.00	333
08/02/99	BIGSTAR ENTERTAINMENT INC	BGST	10	6.94	−31
02/18/99	PINNACLE HOLDINGS INC	BIGT	14	32.56	133
05/10/99	BIZNESSONLINE.COM INC	BIZZ	10	6.84	−32
09/30/99	BLACKROCK INC	BLK	14	18.63	33
09/23/99	BLUESTONE SOFTWARE INC	BLSW	15	58.50	290
07/22/99	BIOMARIN PHARMACEUTICAL INC	BMRN	13	13.31	2
05/24/99	BARNESANDNOBLE.COM INC	BNBN	18	18.13	1
08/02/99	THE BANK OF GODFREY	BOGF	10	10.00	0
03/23/99	ABOUT.COM INC (MININGCO.COM INC) (GENERAL INTERNET INC)	BOUT	25	45.25	81
07/30/99	BIOPURE CORP	BPUR	12	11.00	−8
02/04/99	BRADLEES STORES INC	BRAD	8	8.94	12
05/24/99	BROCADE COMMUNICATIONS SYSTEMS INC	BRCD	19	142.63	651
08/10/99	BRAUN CONSULTING INC	BRNC	7	39.00	457
10/19/99	BSQUARE CORP	BSQR	15	37.94	153
04/20/99	BUCA INC	BUCA	12	11.25	−6
10/05/99	BREAKAWAY SOLUTIONS INC	BWAY	14	57.00	307
06/07/99	BACKWEB TECHNOLOGIES LTD	BWEB	12	30.69	156
05/19/99	CAIS INTERNET INC	CAIS	19	16.13	−15

(continued)

Table 9.1 *Continued*

Offering Date	Company Name	SYMB	Offering Price ($)	12/6/99 Price ($)	Change (%)
07/27/99	AMERICAN NATIONAL CAN GROUP INC	CAN	17	12.75	−25
06/15/99	CAREINSITE INC	CARI	18	61.25	240
02/10/99	CATAPULT COMMUNICATIONS CORP	CATT	10	20.13	101
10/28/99	CAVION TECHNOLOGIES INC	CAVN	6.50	6.88	6
11/03/99	COASTAL BANKING COMPANY INC	CBCO	10	10.25	3
05/11/99	CAREERBUILDER INC	CBDR	13	6.13	−53
08/04/99	COBALT GROUP INC	CBLT	11	8.25	−25
04/22/99	COMPUCREDIT CORP	CCRT	12	31.50	163
03/05/99	CUIDAO HOLDING CORP	CDAO	5.75	5.25	−9
05/05/99	COMPS.COM INC	CDOT	15	6.56	−56
06/02/99	CAPITAL ENVIRONMENTAL RESOURCE INC	CERI	11	6.50	−41
03/31/99	CAPITOL FEDERAL FINANCIAL	CFFN	10	10.00	0
11/18/99	CACHEFLOW INC	CFLO	24	139.88	483
09/22/99	CYBERGOLD INC (CYBER-BUCKS INC)	CGLD	9	9.50	6
10/19/99	CHARLOTTE RUSSE HOLDING INC	CHIC	11	13.75	25
07/12/99	CHINA.COM CORP	CHINA	20	128.31	542
11/08/99	CHARTER COMMUNICATIONS INC	CHTR	19	25.50	34
11/04/99	COLLECTORS UNIVERSE INC	CLCT	6	8.81	47
10/06/99	CALICO COMMERCE INC	CLIC	14	63.38	353
06/30/99	CLARENT CORP (NETIPHONE INC)	CLRN	15	85.06	467
07/26/99	CHEMDEX CORP	CMDX	15	81.94	446
07/21/99	CYBER MERCHANTS EXCHANGE INC DBA C-ME.COM (WORLD WIDE MAGIC NET INC)	CMEE	8	3.00	−63
06/30/99	COMMERCE ONE INC	CMRC	21	345.50	1545
05/12/99	COPPER MOUNTAIN NETWORKS INC	CMTN	21	88.50	321
01/28/99	CNB INC	CNBB	10.25	9.50	−7
04/29/99	CONSOL ENERGY INC	CNX	16	10.25	−36
11/04/99	COBALT NETWORKS INC	COBT	22	139.50	534
02/04/99	CORINTHIAN COLLEGES INC	COCO	18	19.63	9
01/04/99	COHOES BANCORP INC	COHB	10	10.88	9
07/19/99	CONVERGENT COMMUNICATIONS INC	CONV	15	11.44	−24
01/22/99	COVAD COMMUNICATIONS GROUP INC	COVD	18	54.13	201
03/29/99	CRITICAL PATH INC	CPTH	24	65.25	172

Table 9.1 *Continued*

Offering Date	Company Name	SYMB	Offering Price ($)	12/6/99 Price ($)	Change (%)
10/19/99	CROSSROADS SYSTEMS INC	CRDS	18	82.31	357
07/12/99	COMMTOUCH SOFTWARE LTD	CTCH	16	27.50	72
03/18/99	CHEAP TICKETS INC (CHEAPTICKETS.COM)	CTIX	15	12.94	−14
03/05/99	C2 INC	CTOO	4	5.50	38
11/11/99	CVC INC	CVCI	10	13.25	33
01/28/99	CYBEAR INC (1997 CORP)	CYBA	5	7.44	49
06/24/99	CYBERSOURCE CORP	CYBS	11	56.38	413
10/14/99	CYSIVE INC	CYSV	17	52.13	207
05/20/99	DAVIDS BRIDAL INC	DABR	13	9.25	−29
05/12/99	DAG MEDIA INC	DAGM	6.50	3.31	−49
09/30/99	DALEEN TECHNOLOGIES INC	DALN	12	31.94	166
11/08/99	DATA CRITICAL CORP	DCCA	10	14.25	43
11/22/99	DELTATHREE.COM INC	DDDC	15	26.06	74
03/25/99	DELTA GALIL INDUSTRIES	DELT	9.50	17.13	80
05/06/99	DESTIA COMMUNICATIONS INC (ECONOPHONE)	DEST	10	20.50	105
09/30/99	DIGITAL INSIGHT CORP	DGIN	15	41.94	180
11/22/99	DIGITAL IMPACT INC	DIGI	15	60.00	300
07/29/99	DIGEX INC	DIGX	17	45.50	168
05/25/99	DLJDIRECT INC (DONALDSON LUFKIN & JENRETTE)	DIR	20	15.38	−23
06/09/99	DITECH CORP (DITECH COMMUNICATIONS CORP)	DITC	11	107.19	874
02/04/99	DEL MONTE FOODS CO	DLM	15	12.31	−18
03/20/99	DUCATI MOTOR HOLDING SPA	DMH	31.67	27.88	−12
12/01/99	DIGIMARC CORP	DMRC	20	61.44	207
02/04/99	DELPHI AUTOMOTIVE SYSTEMS CORP	DPH	17	15.69	−8
10/27/99	DATA RETURN CORP	DRTN	13	28.63	120
07/27/99	DRUGSTORE.COM INC	DSCM	18	47.44	164
10/05/99	DSL.NET INC	DSLN	7.50	20.88	178
08/06/99	DATALINK CORP	DTLK	7.50	17.38	132
11/10/99	EBOOKERS.COM PLC	EBKR	18	23.00	28
10/25/99	ECTEL LTD	ECTX	12	21.81	82
05/25/99	EDGAR ONLINE INC	EDGR	9.50	7.88	−17
11/10/99	EDISON SCHOOLS INC	EDSN	18	18.06	0
06/28/99	E LOAN INC (ELOAN.COM)	EELN	14	23.06	65
07/14/99	EFFICIENT NETWORKS INC	EFNT	15	73.25	388

(continued)

Table 9.1 *Continued*

Offering Date	Company Name	SYMB	Offering Price ($)	12/6/99 Price ($)	Change (%)
09/28/99	FTD.COM INC	EFTD	8	6.56	−19
09/22/99	EGAIN COMMUNICATIONS CORP	EGAN	12	46.06	284
07/14/99	NATIONAL INFORMATION CONSORTIUM INC	EGOV	12	33.31	178
07/07/99	BORD TELECOM EIREANN (EIRCOM PLC)	EIR	3.99	17.56	340
01/07/99	EUREKA BANK	EKAB	10	8.69	−13
02/01/99	ELDORADO BANCSHARES INC (COMMERCE SECURITY BANCORP INC)	ELBI	9.38	10.13	8
06/02/99	EMUSIC.COM INC (GOODNOISE CORP)	EMUS	35	15.31	−56
11/01/99	ENEL SPA	EN	4.52	44.00	873
07/20/99	ENGAGE TECHNOLOGIES INC	ENGA	15	59.56	297
02/11/99	BOTTOMLINE TECHNOLOGIES INC	EPAY	13	30.75	137
10/14/99	EPCOS AG	EPC	33.41	77.94	133
09/21/99	E.PIPHANY INC	EPNY	16	163.00	919
06/16/99	ESPS INC	ESPS	7.50	4.25	−43
10/08/99	E-STAMP CORP	ESTM	17	35.06	106
01/28/99	ENTERCOM COMMUNICATIONS CORP	ETM	22.50	60.31	168
05/19/99	ETOYS INC	ETYS	20	55.38	177
10/04/99	EVERTRUST FINANCIAL GROUP INC	EVRT	10	9.63	−4
02/22/99	CORPORATE EXECUTIVE BOARD CO	EXBD	19	46.13	143
08/12/99	IXNET INC	EXNT	15	17.50	17
11/09/99	EXPEDIA INC	EXPE	14	50.13	258
04/08/99	EXTREME NETWORKS INC	EXTR	17	70.50	315
05/21/99	FASHIONMALL.COM INC	FASH	13	6.56	−50
04/07/99	FIRST BANCORP OF INDIANA INC	FBEI	10	9.63	−4
01/04/99	FIRST CAPITAL INC	FCAP	10	11.50	15
06/22/99	FIRST COMMUNITY FINANCIAL CORP	FCFN	15	16.88	13
07/27/99	FOCAL COMMUNICATIONS CORP	FCOM	13	25.38	95
08/03/99	FAIRCHILD SEMICONDUCTOR INTERNATIONAL INC	FCS	18.50	33.00	78
05/04/99	FLYCAST COMMUNICATIONS CORP (FLYCAST NETWORK)	FCST	25	79.25	217
07/09/99	FIRST DEPOSIT BANCSHARES INC	FDBI	10	11.38	14
09/27/99	FOUNDRY NETWORKS INC	FDRY	25	242.00	868
04/07/99	FLORIDAFIRST BANCORP	FFBK	10	9.17	−8

Table 9.1 *Continued*

Offering Date	Company Name	SYMB	Offering Price ($)	12/6/99 Price ($)	Change (%)
06/04/99	F5 NETWORKS INC	FFIV	10	117.00	1070
06/24/99	FINANCIAL INSTITUTIONS INC	FISI	14	13.00	−7
03/15/99	FLASHNET COMMUNICATIONS INC	FLAS	17	8.53	−50
08/02/99	1-800-FLOWERS.COM INC	FLWS	21	15.50	−26
10/26/99	LCM INTERNET GROWTH FUND INC	FND	10	10.25	3
11/11/99	FINISAR CORP	FNSR	19	107.00	463
03/04/99	BOYDS COLLECTION LTD	FOB	18	7.69	−57
07/02/99	FPB FINANCIAL CORP	FPBF	10	10.75	8
01/04/99	FIRST PLACE FINANCIAL CORP	FPFC	10	11.69	17
04/26/99	1ST STATE BANCORP INC	FSBC	16	19.81	24
09/27/99	FREESHOP.COM INC	FSHP	12	22.38	86
06/25/99	GREATER ATLANTIC FINANCIAL CORP	GAFC	9.50	5.44	−43
10/28/99	GAIAM INC	GAIA	5	14.00	180
02/10/99	GABELLI ASSET MANAGEMENT (ALPHA G INC)	GBL	17.50	16.81	−4
09/15/99	GARDEN.COM INC	GDEN	12	13.50	13
04/30/99	GENTEK INC	GK	13.75	11.50	−16
09/30/99	GOLDEN TELECOM INC	GLDN	12	11.50	−4
06/17/99	GOTO.COM INC	GOTO	15	80.50	437
03/23/99	GOUVERNEUR BANCORP INC	GOV	5	4.50	−10
05/03/99	GOLDMAN SACHS GROUP INC	GS	53	77.63	46
06/22/99	GLOBESPAN SEMICONDUCTOR INC	GSPN	15	83.50	457
11/22/99	GETTHERE.COM INC	GTHR	16	26.00	63
10/26/99	GREENVILLE FIRST BANCSHARES INC	GVBK	10	10.00	0
07/13/99	HUDSON CITY BANCORP INC	HCBK	10	13.44	34
04/09/99	HUGOTON ROYALTY TRUST (CROSS TIMBERS OIL CO)	HGT	9.50	8.75	−8
08/18/99	HEADHUNTER.NET INC	HHNT	10	15.75	58
09/21/99	HI-Q WASON INC	HIQW	7	3.38	−52
07/06/99	MUSICMAKER.COM INC	HITS	14	7.31	−48
02/10/99	HEALTHEON CORP	HLTH	8	46.44	480
10/07/99	HOMESERVICES.COM INC	HMSV	15	15.00	0
08/04/99	HOMESTORE.COM INC	HOMS	20	74.50	273
07/20/99	HOOVERS INC	HOOV	14	10.56	−25
08/10/99	HOTJOBS.COM LTD	HOTJ	8	33.50	319
06/04/99	HIGH SPEED ACCESS CORP	HSAC	13	22.13	70
04/26/99	HEIDRICK & STRUGGLES INTERNATIONAL INC	HSII	14	27.13	94

(continued)

Table 9.1 *Continued*

Offering Date	Company Name	SYMB	Offering Price ($)	12/6/99 Price ($)	Change (%)
01/21/99	HERSHA HOSPITALITY TRUST	HT	6	5.50	−8
11/09/99	IBASIS INC (VIP CALLING INC)	IBAS	16	38.00	138
01/29/99	PACKAGED ICE INC	ICED	8.50	3.44	−60
08/04/99	INTERNET CAPITAL GROUP INC	ICGE	12	165.19	1277
11/19/99	INTELLI-CHECK INC	IDN	7.50	10.00	33
07/02/99	INDIAN VILLAGE BANCORP INC	IDVB	13.25	11.50	−13
10/04/99	JADE FINANCIAL CORP	IGAF	8	8.50	6
10/13/99	IGO CORP (BATTERY EXPRESS INC)	IGOC	12	20.25	69
06/18/99	INTERSTATE HOTELS MANAGEMENT INC	IHCO	5.23	3.69	−29
08/04/99	INTERNET INITIATIVE JAPAN INC	IIJI	23	123.75	438
06/02/99	IXL ENTERPRISES INC	IIXL	12	38.81	223
05/12/99	INTELLIGENT LIFE CORP	ILIF	13	4.38	−66
10/07/99	ILLUMINET HOLDINGS INC	ILUM	19	51.56	171
11/16/99	IMANAGE INC	IMAN	11	33.38	203
08/25/99	IMAGEX.COM INC	IMGX	7	33.50	379
11/12/99	IMMERSION CORP	IMMR	12	31.63	164
04/27/99	IMMTECH INTERNATIONAL INC	IMMT	10	26.50	165
04/29/99	INFORMATICA CORP	INFA	16	94.00	488
09/23/99	INTERACTIVE INTELLIGENCE INC	ININ	13	26.06	100
07/07/99	INTERLIANT INC (SAGA NETWORKS INC)	INIT	10	20.56	106
02/11/99	INSURANCE MANAGEMENT SOLUTIONS GROUP INC	INMG	11	2.50	−77
07/22/99	INSWEB CORP	INSW	17	26.38	55
05/26/99	INET TECHNOLOGIES INC	INTI	16	68.13	326
06/24/99	INTERNET.COM CORP	INTM	14	35.00	150
08/09/99	INTERWORLD CORP	INTW	15	57.94	286
08/04/99	INTERACTIVE PICTURES CORP	IPIX	18	20.63	15
06/28/99	IQ POWER TECHNOLOGY INC	IQPT	1	1.75	75
06/29/99	DIGITAL ISLAND INC	ISLD	10	57.63	476
09/23/99	INTERSPEED INC	ISPD	12	18.19	52
02/25/99	INTRAWARE INC	ITRA	16	32.88	105
10/26/99	INTERTRUST TECHNOLOGIES CORP	ITRU	18	156.00	767
09/27/99	ITXC CORP	ITXC	12	45.25	277
02/26/99	INVITROGEN CORP	IVGN	15	40.13	168
03/18/99	IVILLAGE INC	IVIL	24	27.25	14
09/23/99	WEBSTAKES.COM INC (NETSTAKES INC)	IWIN	14	9.84	−30
10/07/99	INTERWOVEN INC	IWOV	17	156.13	818
10/19/99	ZAPME! CORP	IZAP	11	9.88	−10

Table 9.1 *Continued*

Offering Date	Company Name	SYMB	Offering Price ($)	12/6/99 Price ($)	Change (%)
07/22/99	JFAX.COM INC	JFAX	9.50	5.56	−41
10/26/99	JNI CORP	JNIC	19	72.00	279
06/24/99	JUNIPER NETWORKS INC	JNPR	34	297.06	774
09/22/99	JORE CORP	JORE	10	12.00	20
10/07/99	JUPITER COMMUNICATIONS INC	JPTR	21	35.00	67
05/25/99	JUNO ONLINE SERVICES INC	JWEB	13	17.00	31
09/21/99	KANA COMMUNICATIONS INC	KANA	15	171.25	1042
09/24/99	KEYNOTE SYSTEMS INC	KEYN	14	71.00	407
02/10/99	KORN/FERRY INTERNATIONAL	KFY	14	23.94	71
12/01/99	THE KNOT INC	KNOT	10	13.88	39
06/08/99	DRKOOP.COM INC (EMPOWER HEALTH CORP)	KOOP	9	17.38	93
11/16/99	KOREA THRUNET CO LTD	KOREA	18	68.25	279
08/18/99	LABRANCHE & CO INC	LAB	14	10.13	−28
05/06/99	LATITUDE COMMUNICATIONS INC	LATD	12	24.25	102
04/22/99	LAUNCH MEDIA INC	LAUN	22	18.00	−18
07/27/99	LIBERATE TECHNOLOGIES	LBRT	16	171.63	973
11/18/99	LIFEMINDERS.COM INC	LFMN	14	20.50	46
07/28/99	LENNOX INTERNATIONAL INC	LII	18.75	11.13	−41
08/19/99	LIONBRIDGE TECHNOLOGIES INC	LIOX	10	21.50	115
04/21/99	LOG ON AMERICA INC	LOAX	10	22.00	120
09/29/99	LOISLAW.COM INC	LOIS	14	30.13	115
08/19/99	LOOKSMART LTD	LOOK	12	35.81	198
07/08/99	LIQUID AUDIO INC	LQID	15	33.38	123
09/15/99	LEISURE TIME CASINOS & RESORTS INC	LTCR	12	9.00	−25
06/09/99	LITRONIC INC	LTNX	11	8.38	−24
09/15/99	LUMINANT WORLDWIDE CORP (CLARANT WORLDWIDE CORP)	LUMT	18	33.38	85
06/17/99	MAIL.COM INC (INAME INC)	MAIL	7	22.44	221
05/11/99	MAKER COMMUNICATIONS INC	MAKR	13	24.63	89
02/10/99	MARINE BANCSHARES INC (COASTAL BANK CORP)	MBSK	10	7.38	−26
12/01/99	MCAFEE.COM CORP	MCAF	12	53.50	346
10/21/99	MCK COMMUNICATIONS INC	MCKC	16	29.00	81
07/08/99	MCM CAPITAL GROUP INC	MCMC	10	3.56	−64
08/04/99	MISSION CRITICAL SOFTWARE INC	MCSW	16	68.63	329
08/11/99	MORTGAGE.COM INC	MDCM	8	8.25	3
07/23/99	ALLSCRIPTS INC	MDRX	16	38.25	139
07/02/99	MEEMIC HOLDINGS INC	MEMH	10	15.50	55

(continued)

Table 9.1 *Continued*

Offering Date	Company Name	SYMB	Offering Price ($)	12/6/99 Price ($)	Change (%)
02/04/99	MICROFINANCIAL INC (BOYLE LEASING TECHNOLOGIES INC)	MFI	15	11.31	−25
07/29/99	MIIX GROUP INC	MHU	13.50	13.13	−3
04/12/99	MIH LTD	MIHL	18	68.38	280
03/29/99	MKS INSTRUMENTS INC	MKSI	14	25.75	84
01/14/99	MARKETWATCH.COM INC	MKTW	17	42.50	150
03/16/99	MULTEX.COM INC (MULTEX SYSTEMS INC)	MLTX	14	27.25	95
02/04/99	MODEM MEDIA POPPE TYSON INC	MMPT	16	60.50	278
05/07/99	MEDIA METRIX INC	MMXI	17	37.13	118
11/19/99	MEDIAPLEX INC	MPLX	12	32.38	170
07/20/99	MP3.COM INC	MPPP	28	38.31	37
04/29/99	MPATH INTERACTIVE INC	MPTH	18	22.94	27
05/03/99	MAPQUEST.COM INC	MQST	15	24.38	63
04/29/99	MARIMBA INC	MRBA	20	37.13	86
09/27/99	MEDSCAPE INC (MEDSCAPE.COM)	MSCP	8	11.63	45
11/17/99	METASOLV SOFTWARE INC	MSLV	19	62.00	226
10/18/99	MARTHA STEWART LIVING OMNIMEDIA INC	MSO	18	29.81	66
11/18/99	METRON TECHNOLOGY NV	MTCH	13	16.00	23
02/16/99	MANNATECH INC	MTEX	8	5.91	−26
12/01/99	METALINK LTD	MTLK	12	22.38	86
08/19/99	MYPOINTS.COM INC	MYPT	8	28.02	250
06/03/99	NETWORK ACCESS SOLUTIONS CORP	NASC	12	23.75	98
10/21/99	NAVISITE INC	NAVI	14	53.38	281
10/13/99	NETCENTIVES INC	NCNT	12	45.25	277
07/28/99	NCRIC GROUP INC	NCRI	7	9.13	30
03/04/99	NEON SYSTEMS INC	NESY	15	24.00	60
05/07/99	NETOBJECTS INC	NETO	12	14.81	23
04/22/99	NET PERCEPTIONS INC	NETP	14	34.25	145
10/14/99	NETRADIO CORP	NETR	11	8.88	−19
11/08/99	NETZEE INC	NETZ	14	14.19	1
10/06/99	NEUBERGER BERMAN INC	NEU	32	25.75	−20
06/29/99	NFRONT INC	NFNT	10	22.69	127
07/27/99	NATIONAL MEDICAL HEALTH CARD SYSTEMS INC	NMHC	7.50	3.44	−54
11/22/99	NDS GROUP PLC	NNDS	20	30.31	52
08/17/99	NOVAMED EYECARE INC	NOVA	8	7.13	−11
06/29/99	NETWORK PLUS CORP	NPLS	16	16.00	0
05/05/99	NORTHPOINT COMMUNICATIONS HOLDINGS INC	NPNT	24	28.00	17

Table 9.1 *Continued*

Offering Date	Company Name	SYMB	Offering Price ($)	12/6/99 Price ($)	Change (%)
07/09/99	NCL HOLDING ASA (NORWEGIAN CRUISE LINES)	NRW	23.78	16.50	−31
09/14/99	NETSILICON INC (NET SILICON) (DIGITAL PRODUCTS INC)	NSIL	7	15.25	118
11/11/99	NETCREATIONS INC	NTCR	13	25.13	93
08/11/99	NETSCOUT SYSTEMS INC	NTCT	11	24.38	122
07/29/99	NETIQ CORP	NTIQ	13	54.25	317
07/29/99	NET2PHONE INC	NTOP	15	54.06	260
08/18/99	NETRO CORP	NTRO	8	28.63	258
09/28/99	NETSOLVE INC	NTSL	13	26.19	101
06/22/99	NETIVATION.COM INC	NTVN	10	6.50	−35
07/29/99	N2H2 INC	NTWO	13	27.25	110
01/21/99	NVIDIA CORP	NVDA	12	38.63	222
05/20/99	NEWGEN RESULTS CORP	NWGN	13	10.25	−21
05/14/99	NEXTCARD INC	NXCD	20	34.63	73
05/17/99	NEXTERA ENTERPRISES INC	NXRA	10	8.00	−20
11/09/99	NEXT LEVEL COMMUNICATIONS INC	NXTV	20	70.13	251
09/23/99	NETZERO INC	NZRO	16	22.44	40
07/14/99	OSWEGO COUNTY BANCORP INC	OCSB	10	9.00	−10
03/24/99	ONEMAIN.COM INC	ONEM	22	18.13	−18
05/18/99	ONESOURCE INFORMATION SERVICES INC (ONESOURCE HOLDING CORP)(DATEXT HOLDING CORP)	ONES	12	12.00	0
02/11/99	ONYX SOFTWARE CORP	ONXS	13	34.00	162
11/22/99	OFFICIAL PAYMENTS CORP (US AUDIOTEX CORP)	OPAY	15	32.88	119
11/22/99	OPENTV INC	OPTV	20	84.38	322
06/03/99	ONLINE RESOURCES & COMMUNICATIONS CORP	ORCC	14	11.13	−21
11/03/99	PAC-WEST TELECOMM INC	PACW	10	23.75	138
06/24/99	QUEPASA.COM INC (INTERNET CENTURY INC)	PASA	12	9.38	−22
01/08/99	PROVIDENT BANCORP INC	PBCP	10	15.94	59
03/30/99	PEPSI BOTTLING GROUP INC	PBG	23	16.88	−27
05/26/99	PRIVATE BUSINESS INC	PBIZ	8	4.50	−44
01/08/99	PEOPLES BANKCORP INC	PBKO	10	11.63	16
03/29/99	PRICELINE.COM INC	PCLN	16	60.75	280
02/04/99	PACIFIC INTERNET LTD	PCNTF	17	42.63	151

(continued)

Table 9.1 *Continued*

Offering Date	Company Name	SYMB	Offering Price ($)	12/6/99 Price ($)	Change (%)
02/25/99	PCORDER.COM INC	PCOR	21	57.00	171
09/27/99	AIRGATE PCS INC (AIRGATE WIRELESS INC)	PCSA	17	46.75	175
10/18/99	PC TEL INC	PCTI	17	44.00	159
07/15/99	PARADYNE NETWORKS INC (PARADYNE CORP)	PDYN	17	30.19	78
02/01/99	PEROT SYSTEMS CORP	PER	16	18.50	16
09/28/99	PERFUMANIA.COM INC	PF	7	14.38	105
11/10/99	PELICAN FINANCIAL INC (PN HOLDINGS INC)	PFI	7	6.75	−4
04/01/99	PFSB BAMCORP INC (PALMYRA SAVINGS)	PFSI	10	9.63	−4
12/01/99	PFSWEB INC	PFSW	17	39.13	130
06/10/99	PHONE.COM INC (UNWIRED PLANET INC)	PHCM	16	157.75	886
07/13/99	PROVANTAGE HEALTH SERVICES INC	PHS	18	9.00	−50
07/01/99	PRIMUS KNOWLEDGE SOLUTIONS INC	PKSI	11	49.75	352
07/27/99	PACKETEER INC	PKTR	15	57.00	280
10/06/99	PLANETRX.COM INC	PLRX	16	19.25	20
10/28/99	PLUG POWER INC	PLUG	15	30.00	100
04/06/99	PLX TECHNOLOGY INC	PLXT	9	18.75	108
10/26/99	PENTASTAR COMMUNICATIONS INC	PNTA	10	15.38	54
11/23/99	PNV INC (PNV.NET INC)	PNVN	17	12.81	−25
09/13/99	PURCHASEPRO.COM INC	PPRO	12	139.63	1064
10/26/99	PREDICTIVE SYSTEMS INC	PRDS	18	45.50	153
05/24/99	PRISM FINANCIAL CORP	PRFN	14	9.75	−30
02/10/99	PRODIGY COMMUNICATIONS INC	PRGY	15	25.56	70
05/05/99	PORTAL SOFTWARE INC	PRSF	14	114.00	714
06/25/99	PERSISTENCE SOFTWARE INC	PRSW	11	13.25	20
10/27/99	LTD	PTNR	13.50	18.69	38
06/08/99	THE PANTRY INC	PTRY	13	8.63	−34
06/30/99	PRIVATEBANCORP INC	PVTB	18	15.25	−15
08/04/99	PIVOTAL CORP	PVTL	12	50.75	323
04/19/99	PROXICOM INC	PXCM	13	78.50	504
07/27/99	QUOKKA SPORTS INC	QKKA	12	9.25	−23
11/15/99	QUINTUS CORP	QNTS	18	51.81	188
03/10/99	NASDAQ 100 TRUST SERIES 1 (NASDAQ GOLD TRUST SERIES 1)	QQQ	102.13	160.20	57
08/12/99	QUEST SOFTWARE INC	QSFT	14	93.50	568

Table 9.1 *Continued*

Offering Date	Company Name	SYMB	Offering Price ($)	12/6/99 Price ($)	Change (%)
10/14/99	QUICKLOGIC CORP	QUIK	10	14.00	40
08/02/99	QUOTESMITH.COM INC	QUOT	11	10.19	−7
06/22/99	RAMP NETWORKS INC	RAMP	11	23.63	115
04/26/99	RAZORFISH INC	RAZF	16	76.25	377
05/17/99	REDBACK NETWORKS INC	RBAK	23	152.63	564
09/29/99	RADWARE LTD	RDWR	18	44.06	145
11/17/99	RETEK INC	RETK	15	66.75	345
08/11/99	RED HAT INC (REDHAT)	RHAT	14	222.75	1491
05/26/99	US CONCRETE INC (RMX INDUSTRIES INC)	RMIX	8	7.38	−8
11/16/99	RAINMAKER SYSTEMS INC	RMKR	8	21.44	168
05/05/99	RADIO ONE INC	ROIA	24	71.25	197
10/05/99	ROME BANCORP INC	ROME	7	6.13	−13
03/08/99	ROWECOM INC	ROWE	16	50.44	215
10/13/99	RESOURCEPHOENIX.COM INC	RPCX	8	15.38	92
01/08/99	RRIDGEWOOD FINANCIAL INC	RSBI	7	6.00	−14
11/11/99	RUDOLPH TECHNOLOGIES INC	RTEC	16	26.13	63
04/06/99	RHYTHMS NETCONNECTIONS INC	RTHM	21	33.06	57
05/21/99	RUBIOS RESTAURANTS INC	RUBO	10.50	7.63	−27
07/15/99	INC	RVST	12	25.44	112
04/09/99	RAVENSWOOD WINERY INC	RVWD	10.50	10.56	1
11/10/99	SAGE INC	SAGI	12	25.69	114
06/30/99	SALEM COMMUNICATIONS CORP	SALM	22.50	16.63	−26
06/21/99	SALON.COM (SALON INTERNET INC)	SALN	10.50	7.25	−31
06/16/99	SBA COMMUNICATIONS CORP	SBAC	9	13.13	46
10/27/99	SPANISH BROADCASTING SYSTEM INC	SBSA	20	35.00	75
07/02/99	SUN COMMUNITY BANCORP LTD	SCBL	16	9.38	−41
07/21/99	SCIENTIFIC LEARNING CORP	SCIL	16	26.25	64
10/21/99	SYCAMORE NETWORKS INC	SCMR	38	248.75	555
05/13/99	SCIENT CORP	SCNT	20	80.25	301
07/09/99	STEELTON BANCORP INC	SELO	10	9.31	−7
04/16/99	STANCORP FINANCIAL GROUP INC	SFG	23.75	28.06	18
01/28/99	SMITH-GARDNER & ASSOCIATES INC	SGAI	12	11.38	−5
04/13/99	SAGENT TECHNOLOGY INC	SGNT	9	22.75	153
10/18/99	SATYAM INFOWAY LTD	SIFY	18	133.97	644
05/05/99	SILKNET SOFTWARE INC	SILK	15	95.13	534
10/05/99	SILICON IMAGE INC	SIMG	12	42.13	251

(continued)

Table 9.1 *Continued*

Offering Date	Company Name	SYMB	Offering Price ($)	12/6/99 Price ($)	Change (%)
02/12/99	SOUTH JERSEY FINANCIAL CORP INC	SJFC	10	14.13	41
11/22/99	SMARTERKIDS.COM INC	SKDS	14	13.00	−7
06/09/99	SKECHERS USA INC	SKX	11	4.13	−63
05/26/99	SALESLOGIX CORP	SLGX	9	31.00	244
06/17/99	STREAMLINE.COM INC	SLNE	10	11.19	12
10/05/99	SMARTDISK CORP (FINTOS INC)	SMDK	13	37.00	185
11/17/99	SYMYX TECHNOLOGIES INC	SMMX	14	29.13	108
06/29/99	SEMINIS INC	SMNS	15	6.19	−59
11/11/99	SOMERA COMMUNICATIONS INC	SMRA	12	19.25	60
10/07/99	SENIOR HOUSING PROPERTIES TRUST	SNH	18	11.75	−35
11/10/99	SONICWALL INC	SNWL	14	36.25	159
08/02/99	SPLITROCK SERVICES INC	SPLT	10	19.25	93
09/28/99	SHOPNOW.COM INC	SPNW	12	21.06	76
09/28/99	SPINNAKER EXPLORATION CO	SPNX	14.50	14.81	2
11/19/99	SCIQUEST.COM INC	SQST	16	36.13	126
06/25/99	US SEARCH CORP.COM	SRCH	9	8.69	−3
02/11/99	SERENA SOFTWARE INC	SRNA	13	29.13	124
08/16/99	SILVERSTREAM SOFTWARE INC	SSSW	16	94.13	488
06/17/99	STUDENT ADVANTAGE INC	STAD	8	21.75	172
06/25/99	STAMPS.COM INC (STAMPMASTER INC)	STMP	11	66.31	503
04/22/99	STATIA TERMINALS GROUP NV	STNV	20	8.75	−56
05/26/99	STARMEDIA NETWORK INC	STRM	15	28.75	92
07/01/99	SUNCOAST BANCORP INC	SUNB	10	14.00	40
06/23/99	SOFTWARE.COM INC	SWCM	15	102.63	584
08/11/99	ANTHONY & SYLVAN POOLS CORP	SWIM	5.50	6.75	23
07/22/99	TANNING TECHNOLOGY CORP	TANN	15	55.25	268
07/19/99	TALK CITY INC (TALKCITY.COM)	TCTY	12	15.50	29
05/21/99	TENFOLD CORP	TENF	17	28.94	70
06/22/99	TEAM FINANCIAL INC	TFIN	11.25	10.38	−8
03/18/99	OUTLOOK SPORTS TECHNOLOGY INC	TGRA	5.80	11.00	90
07/13/99	TIBCO SOFTWARE INC	TIBX	15	106.63	611
09/29/99	TIVO INC	TIVO	16	41.25	158
11/03/99	TICKETS.COM INC (ADVANTIX INC)	TIXX	12.50	20.50	64
07/13/99	THE KEITH COMPANIES INC	TKCI	9	4.75	−47
11/22/99	TELECORP PCS INC	TLCP	20	37.63	88
11/22/99	THE MANAGEMENT NETWORK GROUP INC (TMNG INC)	TMNG	17	30.38	79

Table 9.1   *Continued*

Offering Date	Company Name	SYMB	Offering Price ($)	12/6/99 Price ($)	Change (%)
09/28/99	TELEMATE.NET SOFTWARE INC	TMNT	14	16.88	21
11/02/99	THOMSON MULTIMEDIA GROUP	TMS	22.59	45.38	101
08/05/99	TUMBLEWEED COMMUNICATIONS CORP (TUMBLEWEED SOFTWARE CORP)	TMWD	12	48.00	300
10/27/99	TRITON PCS HOLDINGS INC	TPCS	18	43.13	140
04/30/99	TOWNPAGESNET.COM PLC (TOWN PAGES HOLDINGS PLC)	TPN	10	5.88	−41
06/04/99	TRION TECHNOLOGY AG	TRIN	7	3.50	−50
07/22/99	TROY GROUP INC	TROY	7	13.38	91
11/16/99	TERRA NETWORKS (TELEFONICA INTERACTIVA)	TRRA	13.41	39.94	198
03/31/99	TROY FINANCIAL CORP	TRYF	10	10.94	9
05/10/99	THESTREET.COM	TSCM	19	15.88	−16
04/21/99	TUESDAY MORNING CORP	TUES	15	25.25	68
04/08/99	ITURF INC	TURF	22	17.25	−22
01/28/99	TUT SYSTEMS INC	TUTS	18	41.88	133
03/25/99	TUMBLEWEED INC	TWED	10	5.56	−44
04/07/99	TREX CO INC	TWP	10	27.25	173
05/11/99	TIME WARNER TELECOM INC	TWTC	14	38.25	173
10/07/99	TRIZETTO GROUP INC	TZIX	9	24.88	176
10/06/99	ULTRAPAR PARTICIPACOES SA	UGP	13.50	11.56	−14
10/18/99	RADIO UNICA COMMUNICATIONS CORP	UNCA	16	26.88	68
11/09/99	UNITED PARCEL SERVICE INC (UPS)	UPS	50	65.75	32
08/09/99	US INTERACTIVE INC	USIT	10	37.00	270
04/08/99	USINTERNETWORKING INC	USIX	21	79.75	280
06/16/99	UNITED THERAPEUTICS CORP	UTHR	12	36.50	204
02/10/99	VERTICALNET INC	VERT	16	102.19	539
10/25/99	VIADOR INC	VIAD	9	44.88	399
06/17/99	VIANT CORP	VIAN	16	93.81	486
02/18/99	VIGNETTE CORP	VIGN	19	115.75	509
09/16/99	VITRIA TECHNOLOGY INC	VITR	16	189.00	1081
09/30/99	VIXEL CORP	VIXL	18	35.63	98
02/05/99	VIALOG CORP	VLOG	8	4.00	−50
03/25/99	VALLEY MEDIA INC	VMIX	16	8.06	−50
07/20/99	VOYAGER.NET INC	VOYN	15	10.13	−33
07/23/99	VERSATEL TELECOM INTERNATIONAL NV	VRSA	10.51	29.00	176
11/16/99	VIRATA CORP	VRTA	14	34.38	146

(continued)

Table 9.1 *Continued*

Offering Date	Company Name	SYMB	Offering Price ($)	12/6/99 Price ($)	Change (%)
03/24/99	VARIAN SEMICONDUCTOR EQUIPMENT ASSOCIATES INC	VSEA	8	25.94	224
10/07/99	VITAMINSHOPPE.COM INC	VSHP	11	14.50	32
04/07/99	VALUE AMERICA INC	VUSA	23	11.75	−49
06/29/99	VAXGEN INC	VXGN	13	15.88	22
11/04/99	WEBVAN GROUP INC	WBVN	15	24.38	63
05/11/99	HOLDING CORP) (WESCO DISTRIBUTION INC)	WCC	18	7.69	−57
09/30/99	WILLIAMS COMMUNICATIONS GROUP INC	WCG	23	27.00	17
11/16/99	WEB STREET INC	WEBS	11	14.13	28
02/18/99	WEBTRENDS CORP	WEBT	13	59.88	361
06/28/99	WOMEN FIRST HEALTHCARE INC	WFHC	11	4.75	−57
11/04/99	WIRELESS FACILITIES INC	WFII	15	53.75	258
04/15/99	WORLDGATE COMMUNICATIONS INC	WGAT	21	31.75	51
07/29/99	WATCHGUARD TECHNOLOGIES INC	WGRD	13	25.38	95
08/19/99	WINK COMMUNICATIONS INC	WINK	16	38.84	143
06/03/99	WIT CAPITAL GROUP INC	WITC	9	18.13	101
10/14/99	WOMEN.COM NETWORKS INC	WOMN	10	16.63	66
03/19/99	WORONOCO BANCORP INC	WRO	10	9.75	−3
06/09/99	WAVECOM SA	WVCM	14	44.00	214
10/18/99	WORLD WRESTLING FEDERATION ENTERTAINMENT INC	WWFE	17	16.75	−1
11/19/99	EXACTIS.COM INC (INFOBEAT INC) (MERCURY MAIL INC)	XACT	14	23.50	68
10/04/99	XM SATELLITE RADIO HOLDINGS INC	XMSR	12	26.44	120
06/30/99	THE YANKEE CANDLE COMPANY INC	YCC	18	17.16	−5
09/22/99	YESMAIL.COM INC	YESM	11	17.38	58
06/02/99	ZANY BRAINY INC	ZANY	10	9.00	−10
03/31/99	ZDNET GROUP (ZD NET)	ZDZ	19	21.88	15
05/25/99	ZIPLINK INC	ZIPL	14	11.88	−15
07/19/99	GADZOOX NETWORKS INC	ZOOX	21	77.19	268
11/11/99	ZAP.COM CORP	ZPCM	2	7.75	288
Total Overall Performance for 1999					**148%**

Source: Ostman's Alert-IPO (www.ostman.com) and IPOguys.com.

Table 9.2 IPOguys Return

	% IRR-ROI* (before income taxes)	% Time Wtd. ROI† (before income taxes)
Matthew D. Zito	715.0	769.9
Matt Olejarczyk	273.6	3095.1

* IRR-ROI = Internal Rate of Return – Return on Investment
† Time Wtd. ROI = Time Weighted Return on Investment
Source: Calculations performed by B&R Advisors, Inc. Registered Investment Advisors in Pennsylvania.

changes that we believe are inevitable, and that may ultimately benefit the individual investor. Table 9.2 illustrates how the IPOguys benefited from IPO investing in 1999.

The First Wave of Change—Online Investment Banks

Up to this point, we have focused on the first wave of change that has swept through the financial and investing communities, the shift to online investment banks. This change has opened access to the holy grail of investing—the IPO. The new breed of investment banking has just started to gain footing in the banking industry. Nine current on-line investment banks are highlighted in Chapter 7. By the time this book is printed, there probably will be a few more since Internet time seems to render any facts obsolete in 90 days or less.

How long until the next big change hits the financial and investing community? How long until a brand-new investment vehicle emerges and reveals itself to the individual investor? These are questions that really no one can answer. However, what we do know is this: The Internet is breaking down traditional ways of thinking, traditional structures, and traditional ways of doing business. The Internet is creating enterprises that can expose the inefficiencies and capitalize on the crumbling of these traditional patterns. The Wall Street business model will continue to be significantly impacted as new Internet businesses emerge to exploit and capitalize its inefficiencies. The evolution and transformation of the capital formation process has just begun.

The following are some of our theories, hypotheses, and expectations for the next wave of change that will hit the financial and investing communities. These are the business entities, processes, and scenarios that are likely to be critical in the future.

The Second Wave of Change—The New Online Investment Bank

The second wave of change will evolve around the capital formation process. The Internet will continue to alter the traditional underwriting and distribution processes for allocating shares to the public, and will have a significant impact on the financial and investing communities.

There are already signs that the capital formation process will be a big area where inefficiencies will be exposed and where new businesses will then emerge. Just before we submitted this book to our publisher, three venture capital firms in Silicon Valley—Kleiner Perkins Caufield & Byers, Trident Capital, and Benchmark Capital—have formed a partnership with online brokers Charles Schwab & Co., Inc., TD Waterhouse Group, Inc., and Ameritrade, Inc. The new partnership is forming an online investment bank.

> The online brokers also anticipate distributing exclusively the equity securities underwritten by the new bank once it is operational. The three brokerage firms, the venture partners and the investment bank's management will initially own the company. The new firm, which is yet to be named will be based in Silicon Valley and is expected to be operational in early 2000. It will concentrate on underwriting, managing and distributing equity offerings for information technology and Internet companies.[1]

Just prior to submitting our final manuscript to the publisher in early December 1999, we were able to talk with Scott Ryles, CEO of this new online investment bank. At the time of the interview the investment bank did not have a name or a Web site address, so we will simply call it the "new investment bank."

The new investment bank "will sell securities to not only individual investors but also to institutional clients as well. We will not only sell IPOs, but we will sell other securities consisting of secondary offerings and fixed income securities." The new investment bank will be somewhat similar to E*OFFERING, in that individual investors will have to have accounts at either Charles Schwab, Ameritrade, or TD Waterhouse to have access to buying the IPOs. The new investment bank will exclusively sell to the clients of those three online brokerage firms.

IPOguys: Scott, in the news release above you were quoted as saying, "The company will seek IPO pricing that better reflects the total underlying investor interest in pending IPOs." What do you mean by this statement?

Ryles: IPOs that price at $15.00 a share then trade upwards to 100–300 percent lately are not represented by the individual investor. During the formal offering process the lead manager arranges for institutional investors to meet with the issuer. During the road show the institutional client gets first hand information nonavailable to individuals. This process allows the underwriter to assess the demand for the new issue by institutional investors. The underwriter sets the pricing based on the demand of the institutional buyer and not the individual investor. The individual investor is clearly prepared to buy the shares, but this demand is not reflected by the underwriters to the issuer, because they have no way of gauging individual demand.

This new bank we are developing is about exploiting the Internet technology applied to Wall Street. Wall Street's business model was built on distributing proprietary information to the institutional client. In the world of the Internet, better information can be found collectively instead of from one source. The Internet also distributes information more effectively. The Internet breaks down the value of proprietary information. We exploit the ubiquity of the Web.

Today, 75 percent of the total shares in the technology and Internet stocks that went public in the last 6 months are now owned by individual investors. Institutional clients bought 80 percent of the new issues. Today the institutions own only 25 percent of the total shares.[2]

This new online investment bank is a major step forward to providing more individual investors with IPOs. Considering that the three brokerage houses combined had close to five million accounts as of late 1999, the size of the new online banks alone should help gain them increased leverage in future IPO allocations. The pooling of assets of five million accounts is the equivalent to the financial resources of major institutional investors. With such size and leverage, future new online investment banks should have no trouble gaining access to IPOs for their millions of accountholders.

This unique partnership and new online investment bank that is being built is just the start of what's yet to come in favor of the individual investor. The new online investment banks will help completely change the traditional capital formation process. Three main players stand to benefit from these changes: the new online investment banks, the venture capitalists, and the online individual investor.

New Online Investment Banks

The new online investment bank is the first of the three players that can benefit from the wave of change attacking the inefficiencies of the traditional Wall Street business model. The first example of this bank is the entity formed by Ameritrade, TD Waterhouse, and Charles Schwab. These brokerage houses have been left out of the 1999 underwriting business thus far and have seen millions pass by as the traditional "brick and mortar" underwriters have reaped the benefits of the Internet boom. To get into the game and to start underwriting their own deals, the online brokers have wisely decided to unite in what we refer to as this "new online investment bank." As these brokers forge relationships with venture capitalists, Internet and technology upstarts will be drawn to these new online investment banks to provide traditional underwriting services.

Rather than using traditional underwriting firms, upstarts will benefit by letting this new online investment bank underwrite their offering for a couple of reasons. First, the individual investor is hungry for new issues. With five million or more accountholders there will be plenty of demand and plenty of capital available to buy the issuing stock. Second, the individual investor may be willing to hold these shares longer than traditional institutional investors who often turn-and-burn the stock on the first day of trading. The first 60 days are crucial for upstarts, and there tends to be a longer holding period in the hands of the individual investor compared with the institutional investor. Third, the issuing company will have a direct link to the individual investor, which should lead to more accurate (higher) market valuations over the long term.

These new online investment banks will emerge at an increasing rate. It is only a matter of time before other online brokers, not previously involved in the underwriting process, form new business entities that will allow them to be participants. These new entities will take a piece of the underwriting profits from which they have always been excluded. Other brokerage houses will then start pooling and consolidating their resources to become a part of the lucrative underwriting process. There are over 100 online brokers with the potential to pool together their individual accountholders to replicate the new online investment banking business model. The pooling of these brokers combined with the expertise and backing of venture capitalists looking to form partnerships similar to the Ameritrade, TD Waterhouse, Schwab, VC partnership has the potential to be a major trend impacting the financial and investing community.

The Venture Capitalists

The venture capitalist (VC) is the second of the three players poised to benefit from the wave of change attacking the present Wall Street business model. Traditionally, the VCs provided either seed capital (early-stage cash) or mezzanine capital (later-stage cash) to help bring the upstart to the market. The VC's goal is to steer the upstart toward an initial public offering or hope that the upstart gets acquired. Remember the VC doesn't make money on its original investment until one of the two transactions takes place.

The Internet era is making VCs wealthier by having their investments go public. To further enrich the pot, the VCs now can make money by becoming an underwriter and/or part owner of the underwriting business, in addition to making money as original investors in the deal. This is a way to double-dip for profit. The VC now not only can fund the upstart and profit from the company when it goes public, but also may guide the company through underwriting and keep the entire process in its own back pocket. This concept means the potential for huge profits for the VC, and it also changes the original structure of the company.

This is definitely bad news for the "brick and mortar" under-writers. The VCs could end up taking business away from these tra-ditional investment banks. If our crystal ball is accurate, the VCs are going to steer the companies within which they are invested directly to the new wave of online investment banks in which they have own-ership. The end result could be sweet profits for the VC firms.

The Online Individual Investor

The online individual investor is the third of the three players likely to benefit from the wave of change affecting the Wall Street busi-ness model. The new partnerships between the brokerage houses and the VCs spell opportunity for the individual investor. The new online investment banks see value in the individual investor who, combined with others, can be a strong force in the underwriting process that is revolutionizing the financial industry. The individ-ual investor may never be equal with the institutional investor, but combined under "one roof," individual investors can be a powerful new distribution pipeline for the online investment banks. Individ-ual investors can now command clout. These new entities and part-nerships will increase the flow of allocations in new issues to individual investors. They will get more shares in public offerings primarily because they tend to hold onto allocations in new issues longer than institutional investors.

If we are correct in our opinion that individual investors are less likely to flip shares and are more willing to hold them for the long term, then we definitely see the shift in IPO allocation to the in-dividual investor becoming more prevalent. The upstarts and their original investors will want shares at the issue price in the hands of individual investors, who are less likely to sell the shares over the short term. A decrease in the sell side of the equation leads to price stabilization of the new issue, which is the ultimate goal of the un-derwriting process. This will help direct future underwriting deals toward the new online investment banks that allocate shares to the individual investor. We truly believe the individual investor will be one of the most influential factors in the underwriting process within the next 1 to 5 years. With the cooperation of online invest-ment banks, we plan to conduct studies on the length of time in-vestors hold new issue shares and will make our findings available on the IPOguys.com Web site.

As an individual investor, it will be important to align yourself as an investor with the "new" online investment banks and current online investment banks that sell shares in IPOs to individuals. This may entail having brokerage accounts at 5 to 10 companies. In Chapter 7, we highlighted the nine companies that currently exist. Probably by the time this book appears, there will be two or three more. As a shrewd, educated, and responsible investor, it will be your job to keep up with all the opportunities that become available in the next few years. We can help you here. It is the mission of the IPOguys to keep you informed of ongoing changes in the coming years. The IPOguys are individual investors, just like you, who plan on profiting from these new opportunities that develop. As individual investors, we plan to be in the forefront of the revolution, and in sharing these insights with you.

Third Wave of Change—Chaos: The Individual Investor Will Rule

No matter how hard anyone fights it, the outcome is inevitable. Everything the Internet touches results in the empowerment of the individual to dictate pricing, terms, and conditions. The financial and investment communities will not be an exception. The online individual investor will rule the future of finance in America.

We conclude this chapter by discussing some of the major developments that are impacting, or going to impact, the financial and investing communities. Some of our comments may seem a little radical, but that is what the Internet is all about, chaos. The speed and significance of change in the financial and investment community lead us to think that some of our ideas will materialize in the next 5 to 10 years. These ideas are always about empowering the individual investor. We hope you will enjoy reading about them and that a few of them will become reality.

The Online Individual Investor Buying Combine
The first of three developments that may impact the financial and investing communities is the concept of the "buying combine." The biggest deterrent to this concept will be the SEC, and the laws that govern the buying and selling of securities in our country. In this section, we take a look at what we mean by "buying combine."

Today we have online investment banks like Wit Capital, FBR, and Einvestmentbank.com. By regulation, these firms are "broker dealers." They are registered with the SEC and all the exchanges. These online investment banks legally can buy and sell securities to individuals, trade the shares on NASDAQ, issue IPOs to individuals, and provide similar services to their clients.

As individual investors become more empowered, new entities (buying combines) will be created that are owned or operated by these investors. Instead of the online investment bank controlling the distribution of shares to clients, the buying combine as a whole will decide together in true democratic fashion. Instead of the online investment bank deciding which clients will get shares, the combine will decide. The members of the buying group—all individual investors with equal say—may dictate together as a group which investments to take part in by voting. All this communication between investors will be done via e-mail and through customized personal Web pages. Together, the group will decide what investments to pursue; then the individual investors can choose whether or not to participate. Each individual who participates may have an equal ownership of that security, or issue. No one member may have rights to more shares or a larger allocation than other members. The powerful buying group accomplishes two things:

1. As a group, the individual investors dictate terms, price, and allocations. The individual investor controls and makes decisions based on his or her own investment choice. Today's investment vehicles are dictated and controlled by the owners who sell them. You can buy into a mutual fund, you can buy a stock through a broker, but it's hard to buy a security for yourself. You have to be represented by some sort of entity that is going to make money off your transaction. Why in the future couldn't individuals pool together as equals, and make huge buying decisions like traditional mutual funds, online brokers, and brokerage houses? The closest relative to the buying combine concept is called DRPs, short for direct reinvestment plans. These are plans set up by individual companies so that individual investors can buy shares of a company stock directly through the

company, bypassing the traditional broker or brokerage house. If you can buy stock from a company directly, then why could you not in the future buy stock at the issue price from the issuing company?

2. The buying combine and its members equally may get the same amount of allocation. This might never happen but the process would be better and fairer than it is today.

We are not sure of the legal and government regulations that may or may not allow such an entity to exist. Today's SEC laws probably would forbid such an entity, but in the future this may change. Since the main mission of the SEC is to regulate the securities industry so it is fair to investors, the Commission will indeed level the playing field for individual investors and permit the development of buying combines in some form or another.

Hundreds of "angel investment groups" are being formed all around the country. Former entrepreneurs, executives, and wealthy individuals are pooling together their own money to provide seed capital to upstarts. These angel groups are acting as venture capitalists. Instead of being private for-profit corporations, these clubs are forming limited partnerships and other kinds of entities. Some angel groups are very informal in their structure allowing the group members to make individual investments no matter what the group decides to do. The point we are making is that many high-wealth individuals are already coming together as investment groups. We are not aware that they are using the Internet yet to distribute shares or equity, but they may in the future. If high-wealth individuals are forming informal less restrictive buying groups, why can't individual investors pool together and form legal structured investing entities?

The Internet is spawning global competitiveness, and buying combines already are being formed in the retail industry. Internet companies are forming to help both individuals and businesses join together to reduce costs by buying products and services in bulk. As a group, they are buying hundreds or thousands of products and services from one vendor. The bulk purchase decreases the overall cost for each individual or company, thus, saving money for each member of the buying group on every transaction. This new entity is how we envision individual investors coming together as a group and leveling the playing field. This is a powerful theory. The IPOguys are committed to seeking out and developing such an entity for the future of the individual investor. We welcome any reader's comments or ideas and have developed a section on the IPOguys.com Web site for your feedback. You can post your ideas and comments on the "buying combine" bulletin board. We want to make it clear that this is just an idea, not an offer to join or sell anything. Being committed to the individual investor, we anticipate that the content in the IPOguys.com Web site will mainly be dictated and built ultimately by you, the reader and individual investor. We want to create a forum and voice for your opinions, comments, and decisions.

24-Hour Global Stock Market

The second development affecting the financial and investing communities is the 24-hour global stock market. In the future, there will be a global stock market, open 24 hours a day, seven days a week, allowing individual investors to buy and sell securities both domestically and globally every day of the year. The United States will be instrumental in this movement and will be the first to combine all the major indexes together. The day may soon come when the NASDAQ-Amex and New York exchanges are linked together via electronic computers providing trading to individual investors both day and night. Already smaller ECNs (electronic computer networks) are being built to provide investors after-hours trading, prior to 9:30 A.M. and after 4:30 P.M. The New York Stock Exchange is also talking about going public sometime in the near future. This is a sign that the traditional walls are being broken down and that the reality of one exchange is not too far behind.

One exchange, or a linking of the two major exchanges, might occur in the next 3 to 5 years. When the one-exchange concept will materialize will depend on government regulation and approval, and may take as long as 10 years. But a 10- to 15-year time frame is what we estimate it will take to achieve a global marketplace that links all international exchanges in some form or another. Again, the timing depends on U.S., as well as foreign, government regulations. However, the Internet and technology innovations should make it a reality sometime in our lifetime.

The IPO Road Show

The third development impacting financial and investing communities is the opening of the doors to the IPO road show, the promotional tour that has been an integral part of the traditional underwriting process. When an issuing company wants to go public, it needs to meet with the potential buyers of the issuing shares. After the issuing company files with the SEC and prior to the pricing of the issue, the issuing company holds meetings at major cities across the country. The executives of the issuing company meet with the managers of mutual funds, insurance companies, pension plan managers, and with private individuals who will buy the issuing shares at the issue price. The meetings are basically the "pitch" or "sales promotion": Executives of the issuing company explain the business to the potential buyers. The potential buyers are "institutional investors" who traditionally buy up to 80 percent of the issuing shares. The institutional investors are the major players on Wall Street. Many are the managers of mutual funds you currently own in your other investment portfolios. The road show meetings take place behind closed doors. The general public or individual investors are not invited. The SEC does not allow individual investors to attend because they believe that the "general" investing community may not be accurately represented, and that the information conducted inside these meetings is too sophisticated for the individual investor. However, we are sure that thousands maybe even millions of individual investors are just as competent as some institutional investors. Protecting the average investor from buying a piece of the "blue sky" is another main reason the SEC does not allow the individual investor access to the road show. Finally, the institutional investors' assets are much greater than those of your average individual investor so the SEC does not really concern itself with the institutional investor. Once the road show meeting is over, the institutional investors leave the meeting and shortly thereafter place their conditional offers to buy the issuing stock with their "dealer/brokers."

The Internet, and the emergence of the individual investor will change this process. In December 1999, Charles Schwab received a letter from the SEC stating that Charles Schwab may give their individual accountholders access to the road shows via the Schwab.com

Web site. Charles Schwab stated that they were going to give accoun-tholders with a minimum of $100,000 in their accounts access to road shows. These investors then would be given first priority to buy IPOs underwritten by Charles Schwab. Just as in traditional invest-ment banking, the accountholders with the most money get the first opportunities. We salute Charles Schwab for undertaking this task and allowing individual investors a seat in the road show. Though the individual investors may not be in the meetings physically, they will be allowed to view the road show via the Internet. Using audio and video through the Internet, individual investors will be able to have their seat right in front of their computer.

This is just the beginning. Eventually, the underwriting pro-cess will include more individual investors, and the road show will include any individual investor without any bias toward the amount of money he or she has as assets.

That's All, Folks

We hope we have adequately prepared you for IPO investing via the Internet. More importantly, we hope we have broadened your think-ing so that you may recognize and profit from future investing op-portunities. For now, you should probably focus on making your first successful IPO trade. IPOs can be a great investment vehicle for the online individual investor and will only improve into the foreseeable future. Don't be surprised if IPO allocations to online individual investors reach 50 percent of the total allocation pie in the next 5 to 10 years. When you see a headline in the *Wall Street Journal* proclaiming, "IPO Allocations to Individual Investors Reach 50 Percent," remember that you read it here first. Best wishes to you, the online individual investor, in your financial success.

No matter how hard anyone fights it, the outcome is in-evitable. The online individual investor will rule the future of fi-nance in America.

Summary

- Stay on top of developments that will create new opportuni-ties for the individual investor. The move of the individual investor to online banks was the first wave of change. The opening of access to IPOs was the benefit of this change.

- The second wave that will occur in the financial and investing communities is the ongoing evolution and radical transformation of the capital formation process and the breakdown of the inefficient Wall Street business model. The three players that will benefit from this change are the online brokers, the venture capital firms, and the online individual investor.

- The third wave of change will be the complete shift of power to the individual investor. Three potential outcomes include the formation of buying combines, the 24-hour global stock market, and the opening of the road show to individual investors.

appendix

traditional discounting
of ipo shares

The following analogy illustrates how and why IPO shares may be initially discounted.

During his spare time, Dr. Craig buys and fixes up houses for a living. He has found two nice "fixer-up" properties located in a section of town that is just beginning to boom. Since he is willing to take the risk of being one of the first developers in the area, he can buy both properties for a discounted price of $80,000 total. Once he fixes these two homes up, he believes they will be worth $150,000 total because he is confident in the growth of that section of town. Realizing what a sweet deal this is, Dr. Craig feels under pressure to make his offer to the seller before the competition finds out about these two houses and beats him to the punch.

His main problem is that he does not have $80,000 readily available to buy the two properties. Understandably, what is most important to Dr. Craig right now is to come up with $80,000 very quickly so that he can get in ahead of the competition. So he decides to sell another property that he has completed restoring, with the hope he can come up with the $80,000.

Dr. Craig bought this property a year ago for $70,000, but it is currently valued at $100,000, which he thinks is a fair market price.

To ensure he can move the restored house on the market quickly and before the competition buys those other two homes, he decides to sell the restored home at a discounted price of $85,000. This is a little bit more than the $80,000 that he actually needs—enough to buy the other two properties with some cash to spare. Coincidentally, the sale price of $85,000 calculates as a 15 percent discount to the actual market value of $100,000.

The preceding scenario illustrates what may happen during the IPO process and highlights some interesting similarities to current market conditions:

- House is located in a section of town that is just beginning to boom.
- The new issue is located in a sector of the economy that is beginning to boom.

- Since Dr. Craig is willing to risk being one of the first developers in the area, he has the opportunity to purchase both properties at a discounted price of $80,000.
- Since IPO investors are willing to risk investing in the typically young, new issue companies, they typically have the opportunity to purchase IPO shares at a discounted price of 15 percent.

- Dr. Craig believes the two houses will be worth $150,000 total because he is confident in the growth of that section of town.
- IPO investors believe the new issue company will be worth significantly more because they are confident in the growth of that sector (the Internet).

- Realizing what a sweet deal this is, Dr. Craig wants to make his offer to the seller before the other competition finds out about these two houses and beats him to the punch.
- Realizing the opportunity, the private company wants to get the product/service to market before the competition beats it to the punch.

- Dr. Craig does not have $80,000 readily available to use to buy the two properties at this time.

- The private company does not have the necessary capital available to grow at this time.

- Dr. Craig urgently needs to come up with $80,000 to get in ahead of the competition.
- The private company urgently needs to come up with a lot of money to beat the competition to the market.

- So Dr. Craig decides to sell another property that he has completed restoring.
- So the new private company decides to do an IPO and sell stock (ownership in the company) to investors.

- Dr. Craig has decided to sell the restored property he bought a year ago for $70,000; it is now valued at $100,000, which he thinks is a fair market price.
- The private company valuation is difficult to determine using traditional measures. The private company is being valued at what those who performed due diligence have agreed is a fair market value.

- To ensure that the house sells on the market quickly and before the competition beats him to the punch on those other two homes, Dr. Craig decides to sell the restored home at a discounted price of $85,000.
- To ensure success in raising the necessary capital, the private company agrees to let the underwriter price the IPO for market, so long as the new company gets the necessary cash, before the competition beats them to the punch.

- This is a little bit more than the $80,000 that Dr. Craig actually needs—enough to buy the other two properties with some to spare.
- IPOs raise a predetermined amount of capital for the new issuing company, maybe with a little to spare.

- Coincidentally, the sale price of $85,000 calculates to a 15 percent discount to the actual market value of $100,000.

- Coincidentally, the average IPO has been historically under-priced by about 15 percent.

Other Analysis for Thought:

- The price placed on the house may not represent its real value (i.e., the house is valued at $100,000 but is priced at $85,000).
- The new issue price of a company going public may not necessarily represent its value.

- Underpricing the house provides incentive for homebuyers to purchase the house quickly, which achieves the ultimate goal of raising capital for Dr. Craig.
- Underpricing a new issue provides incentive for investors to purchase shares quickly, which achieves the ultimate goal of raising capital for the company going public.

- From the homebuyers' perspective, this is getting a great deal. They have the opportunity to buy the restored house at a significant discount. They can resell the restored house at market value the very next day for a profit of $15,000 if they so desire.
- From the IPO investors' perspective, this is a great deal. They have the opportunity to buy the initial shares at a significant discount. They can resell the IPO shares at market value the very next day if they so desire.

- Whether the house is properly priced can be argued without end. Without incentive, the house may not sell quickly enough.
- Whether these shares are properly priced can be argued without end. Without incentive, the public may never buy the shares.

- Valuation of the house and determination of the offering price are two completely different things. Setting the price is a result of what the market will bear as much as it is a factor of valuation.

- Valuation of a company and determination of the offering price are two completely different things. Setting the price is a result of what the market will bear as much as it is a factor of valuation.

- The art of determining what the market will bear and creating scarcity or the perception of scarcity is the true value and power of Dr. Craig. Who is controlling the deal? Think about that one for a minute.
- The art of determining what the market will bear and creating scarcity or the perception of scarcity is the true value and power of the lead underwriter. Who is controlling the deal? Think about that one for a minute.

- Everybody involved in the preceding equation wins.
- Everybody involved in the preceding equation wins.

epilogue

ipo surgeon general's warning

The following is a narrative of a typical scene when the phone call arrives or the alarm goes off, signaling it is time to place my order for the hottest new IPO available.

Do not try this at home if you have a serious medical condition or ailment. The level of excitement you'll experience investing in IPOs might just be too much for the "faint-at-heart."

"Ring, ring . . . ring, ring" the phone beckons. My full attention turns to that little red flashing light and hypnotizing bell. Whenever the phone rings these days, my curiosity overflows since the incoming call might be just the one I am waiting for.

As I pick up the phone, I wonder whether it could be "the call" since it is the correct time of day for it. Before I can even finish the standard greeting, "Hel . . . ," a voice interrupts. Immediately I know this is "the call" since the higher than normal pitch and tone of voice on the other end of the line steals the conversation, beginning it and ending it with only these three words . . . "Freakin' Hit It."

Any activity that existed in the room prior to the phone ringing takes on a white haze, and becomes a complete blur. I have just entered a completely new space and time. My stomach rises to the top of my throat as my chest fills with air. My hand frantically searches for the base unit as I reach to hang up the phone.

As soon as the phone reaches its home, I notice my other hand has reflexively found the mouse, and in less than three seconds, the pointer has found the proper bookmark. My free hand finds the Enter key and then reaches for the telephone receiver and presses the speed dial button curiously labeled "F.H.I." The Web site loading onto the screen draws the bulk of my attention while the ringing in my ear distracts the rest. "I wish they would pick up the phone already."

Finally, the ringing stops. The brief moment of silence between when the ringing stops and the person on the other end of the line mutters the first word seems like an eternity. As he begins his standard greeting, I feel the muscles in my neck and face tighten as my voice shifts to a higher pitch, and I excitedly proclaim in my best falsetto . . . "Freakin' Hit It."

No response on the other end is necessary as both phones simultaneously hang up. My eyes race back and forth between the keyboard and the screen as my fingers play an intense concerto across the keys. It is critical that my keystrokes are perfect and error free and exactly match my intended results.

Punching one letter at a time, I successfully complete field after field, screen after screen. "This is taking far too long," I say to myself. "I should be much faster at this by now. Come on, let's go!!! Be careful though, no mistakes, or you'll have to start all over again. All right now, take a big breath . . . deep breath . . . calm down . . . now exhale. Ahhhh. Okay. Better. Just a few more keystrokes . . . there . . . done."

Thoughts race through my mind as I make one final review before submitting the information. On thorough inspection, everything looks correct, so I cautiously press the Enter key, then watch the final screen appear.

I attempt to write down my confirmation number but have difficulty holding onto the pen. The cold sweat on my palms is the first sign that I am emerging from "the zone."

External influences now begin to reach my conscious mind. A distant muttering sound is tuning in, becoming louder, closer, and clearer. The frequency is familiar. It is the sound of a human voice, originating in the other room.

Merging my "inner distance" with my external surroundings is going to take a focused effort. Using every bit of mental energy I can summon up, I slowly turn my head to the right. My eyes don't follow though, still fixated on the computer monitor. So I close them for a moment, and reopen them to notice some shuffled papers sitting on the desk. It appears that the audio senses are back, but the sense of sight is still lost somewhere.

I close my eyes again and lift my head. My eyelids feel like 20,000-pound steel doors blanketing my eyes shut. I command them to open, and they forcefully and gradually obey.

The white-hazed frame in front of me slowly comes into focus, and at last I recognize it is an open doorway about six feet in front of me. I also notice the photo on the wall of the soaring eagle in my peripheral vision just off to the left.

I am finally beginning to realize where I am, and what just occurred. My mind and body have just reentered present space and time, directly from the zone. Now that I have regained consciousness, I am able to appreciate the hurricane that just entered the room by way of that last telephone call. Only three minutes have actually passed, although it feels as if it's been at least a half hour.

I take a moment and chuckle at my level of excitement, and sit amazed at how my mind and body still respond when the call arrives, even after all this time . . . to those three simple, yet powerful words . . . "Freakin' Hit It."

Those three little words conjure up a level of excitement that can only be matched through intense athletic competition or through basic survival reflexes. The adrenaline rush certainly is comparable to anything you can ever experience.

Those three words have become as common a saying to us as Nike's "Just Do It" or Jerry McGuire's "Show Me the Money." Why? Because these words truly do show us the money. Those three words have meant substantial profits to my colleagues and me over the past year.

Freakin' Hit It are the three sweetest, most desirable words in our vocabulary. Not very complex, but very effective. I don't know if my mind and body will ever respond calmly to the sound of a ring-ing telephone, followed by those three words.

I sometimes hear a distant ringing when I'm working in the yard, or sitting in a seminar, then notice my posture straighten and my blood pressure rise. Occasionally, my colleagues enjoy getting a rise out of me by exclaiming those three words in their own distinct falsettos. All kidding aside, however, we have all come to respect those three words. As with the boy tending sheep who cried wolf too many times . . . there is no joking around with those three words . . .

If your sole investment objective is conservative growth or stability, we advise you to stay with bonds, CDs, or the like. How-ever, if you are looking to take control of your financial future and are ready to commit a portion of your investment toward an ag-gressive growth strategy, then read this poem . . . and get ready to Freakin' Hit It.

Ode to the IPO . . . Am I Ready?
(A Poem, and Reflection)

I'm fresh as an apple,
just picked off the tree

Cool as some orange juice,
freshly squeezed just for me

Excited as a child,
the first time at the zoo

As ready to freakin' hit it,
as a black belt in Shorei-Ryu

Hit It!!!!!! Kia!!!!!!

notes

chapter 1   the internet investing revolution

1. *Fortune* magazine (October 11, 1999), p. 120.
2. "The Internet," *Wall Street Journal* (December 6, 1999), p. R32.

chapter 2   ipos, the new investment vehicle

1. "Now, Big Institutional Investors Gripe over IPO Allocations, Too," *Wall Street Journal* (November 19, 1999), p. C16.

chapter 3   ipo performance

1. *The New American Webster Handy College Dictionary* (New York: Penguin, 1981), p. 287.

chapter 5   preinvesting preparation and research

1. Kenan Pollack, Hoover's IPO Central, e-mail interview by Matt Zito (August 23, 1999).
2. Larry Kramer, CEO, CBS.Marketwatch.com, e-mail interview by Matt Zito (October 30, 1999).
3. Ben Holmes, President, ipoPros.com, phone interview by Matt Zito (August 12, 1999).
4. Renaissance Capital, IPOhome.com, e-mail interview by Matt Zito (August 12, 1999).
5. David Menlow, IPO Financial Network, phone interview by Matt Zito (November 8, 1999).
6. John J. DeFalco, President, ipodata.com, e-mail interview by Matt Zito (September 8, 1999).
7. *Business 2.0,* quote from Editor-in-Chief (August 1999), p. 1.
8. Tom Taulli, Internet Analyst, e-mail interview by Matt Zito (December 28, 1999).
9. Dr. Irv DeGraw's biography, WorldFinanceNet.com, Web page.

10. Francis Gaskins' biography, Gaskins IPO Desktop, Web page.

11. Rob Zimmer, Director, RadioWallStreet.com, e-mail and phone interview (November 23, 1999).

12. John Fitzgibbon, Internet Analyst with Redherring.com, e-mail interview (November 24, 1999).

chapter 6   getting started

1. Ben Holmes, phone interview (November 24, 1999).

2. "Money and Investing," *Wall Street Journal,* (October 26, 1999), p. C1.

chapter 7   where to buy ipos

1. Friedman, Billings, Ramsey & Co., Inc., Web page (August 27, 1999).

2. Friedman, Billings, Ramsey & Co., Inc., Web page (December 13, 1999).

3. Bill Hambrecht and Sharon Smith, WR Hambrecht + Co., e-mail interview (December 3, 1999).

4. Jennifer Cross, E*OFFERING, e-mail interview (November 18, 1999).

5. einvestmentbank.com, home page, Web site (August 16, 1999).

6. IPOSyndicate.com, home page, Web site (August 16, 1999).

chapter 9   ipos and the future for online individual investors

1. TD Waterhouse press release (San Francisco: November 15, 1999).

2. Scott Ryles, CEO, "New Investment Bank," phone interview (December 3, 1999).

ipoguys terminology

Buying Combine Individuals pooling their purchases together to reduce the cost of each purchase for the individual in the combine. Individual investors may pool their money together in the near future, creating a huge buying machine in the securities markets.

Hammer Down Another term for hitting it.

Hit It The act of placing conditional offers in Internet-related IPOs.

Hitting It Researching, developing trading strategies, working hard to improve your overall rate of return on your investments; striving to ultimately increase your total portfolio; your mission to make money.

IPOguy Symbolizes the spirit of the online individual IPO investor. He is out there every day, hammering away, fighting for access to the golden egg of investing, the IPO.

Iron Gut The measure of strength, willpower, and discipline to withstand tremendous market volatility.

IPOguys Mission A commitment to help online individual investors get access to IPOs and other premier investing opportunities.

ipo glossary

Allocation   The process of distributing new issues or IPOs to investors. If your conditional offer is accepted by the online investment bank, then you will be "allocated" shares in the offering.

Brick and Mortar   Traditional businesses that have not seen the Internet as the wave of the future. They generally have storefront assets.

Capital Formation Process   The process issuing companies go through to raise capital, from filing with the SEC to seeing the shares publicly trade on one of the U.S. exchanges.

Compounding   A calculation of reinvesting money over time. Compounding is significant when you can achieve consistent returns multiple times.

Conditional Offer   A commitment or offer to buy shares in an initial public offering. You can cancel, or change your offer anytime prior to the offering becoming effective.

Confirmation   Your recommitment, or a firm order to buy a new issue at the offering price. Generally, investors "reconfirm" their conditional offer. This is the last step you take in buying a new issue.

Diversification   Spreading out your investment risk over multiple investments.

E-Investor   Educated and informed, strategic and wise, disciplined and thorough (careful in planning). This new breed of investor uses the Internet and online investment banks for investing, including buying and selling IPOs online; also known as the online individual investor.

ECNs   Electronic computer networks that link buy and sell stock orders. Most of today's ECNs are providing the after-hours trading that currently takes place.

Expert Information   Qualified information from reliable sources generally distributed by the media.

Flipping   The act of making a quick profit from selling an IPO within an established minimum number of days. Most underwriters discourage flipping in an effort to protect the stock price and limit the risk of the stock falling below the IPO price. Many underwriters have implemented rules that hinder a flipper's chances of getting future allocations.

Green Shoe   Also commonly referred to as the over allotment. These are the additional shares the underwriter can negotiate to buy from the issuing company. A percentage of shares in excess of the original total underwriting amount issued.

Gross Spread   The commission and fees for underwriting the issue. The difference between the price the lead underwriter and syndicate members pay for the initial shares and the price at which they resell those shares to the institutional and individual investors. Also known as the underwriter's discount.

Hot IPO   A new issue that Wall Street and experts in the IPO investment community believe will increase greatly in price from the issue price to the first-day opening.

Individual Investor   Educated and informed, strategic and wise, disciplined and thorough (careful in planning). The new breed of investor who uses the Internet and online investment banks for investing, including buying and selling IPOs online. Also known as the E-investor.

Information-Based Economy   The concept that the global economy is becoming increasingly dependent on the efficient exchange of information. The new economy of the millennium.

Institutional Investor   Traditionally, a mutual fund company, insurance company, local or state government, a university or college, a wealthy family or wealthy individual. Assets generally exceed $1,000,000.

Internet Investing Revolution   The shift of power from the traditional "old boys" brokerage houses on Wall Street to the individual investor.

Investment Vehicle   A method of putting one's money to profitable use. When we refer to the new investment vehicle, we are referring to IPOs, the newest investment vehicle for the online individual investor.

IPO (initial public offering)   The issue and sale of a stock to the public for the first time; new issue securities.

IPO Pipeline The term used to define the list of companies that have filed registration statements with the SEC but have not yet gone public.

Lead Underwriter (lead manager) The underwriter in charge of establishing the offering price and allocating the shares to all the underwriters involved in the deal.

"Lockup" Period The time period when officers and other major shareholders in the newly public company are restricted from selling shares, usually 180 days.

Moonshot An IPO that makes disproportionately large gains in stock price on the first day of trading. With stocks, the bar has been raised to only include stocks that double of triple in value on the first day of trading. This term is also loosely used to describe any stock that makes incredibly large price leaps during a trading session.

NYSE Acronym for the New York Stock Exchange, the largest exchange in the United States, where many of the biggest companies' stocks are bought and sold. Most traditional blue chip stocks are bought and sold on the NYSE.

NASDAQ Acronym for the National Association of Securities Dealers Automated Quotation System. Most of the Internet companies today are bought and sold on NASDAQ. NASDAQ does not have a trading floor like the NYSE. All stocks are traded through a network of computers.

New Issue Another name for an initial public offering.

Offering Price The price at which shares will be sold to IPO investors. The lead underwriter sets this price.

Online Individual Investor Educated and informed, strategic and wise, disciplined and thorough (careful in planning). The new breed of investor who uses the Internet and online investment banks for investing, including buying and selling IPOs online. Also known as the E-investor.

Online Investment Bank A firm specializing in selling securities to individuals via the Internet. Online investment banks sell shares in new issue to individual investors. Online investment banks also offer traditional brokerage services.

Opening Price The price at which the IPO starts trading on the open market. On occasion, there may be a great disparity between the offering price and the opening price.

Overallotment   The deal made by underwriters with the issuing company to buy additional shares of the company stock at the initial price. The overallotment is typically between 10 and 15 percent. Also commonly referred to as "Green Shoe."

Paper Trade   Trading real stocks "on paper" or "for pretend," with "pretend money" and a "pretend account." This is a highly recommended strategy for getting comfortable with any form of individual investing.

Preliminary Prospectus   Also known as the red herring, the same document as the prospectus. However, it does not contain price information or the offering date. The document gets its name from the red ink on the first page stating that the document is not an official offer to sell securities.

Primary Market   Where IPOs are initially sold, prior to the "secondary" (or open) market.

Prospectus   A condensed version of the registration statement that details a new issue security. The prospectus provides the potential investors with a complete analysis of the potential risks associated with investing in the registered company.

Quiet Period   An SEC-mandated period of 25 days from the day of the first trading date of an IPO where the company and underwriter are extremely limited in information they can release to the public. This quiet period protects the investor from the company and underwriter overhyping the IPO.

Red Herring   The term or slang word used to describe the prospectus in its initial version, printed without the price of the issue and its effective date.

Registration Statement   A lengthy document filed with the SEC containing pertinent facts about the firm planning to sell new securities. Also known as the S-1 statement.

Road Show   The introduction of the company preparing for an IPO to the syndicate, institutional investors, analysts, and other potential clients. These meetings are by invitation only and generally take place behind closed doors in major cities across the United States prior to the company going public.

S-1 Statement   A document filed with the Securities Exchange Commission (SEC) by a company desiring to go public. Also known as the registration statement.

Secondary (Open) Market   Also known as the Wall Street Floor, a place where a stock is actively being traded to the general public.

Securities and Exchange Commission (SEC)   The federal government agency responsible for overseeing the issue of new securities and for enforcing the Securities Act of 1933.

Settlement Date   The date at which an IPO transaction is officially complete. The date at which the money officially changes hands.

Silicon Alley   Nickname for section of New York City where high-tech companies and funding are increasing at a rapid pace. Name mimics Silicon Valley in California.

Silicon Valley   The regional hub in California where a majority of the high-tech companies in the United States are founded. The valley got its name from the start-up computer chip companies that were formed in the 1970s. Computer chips at that time were made from silicon.

Spinning   Distribution of IPO shares to friends and family members, or to venture capitalists, executives, or other special parties.

Trade   The business of buying and selling.

Trade Date   The actual day on which an individual investor either buys or sells shares of equity.

Underwriter   A firm whose business is buying shares from the issuing companies and then reselling the shares to the public.

Underwriting   The process that investment banks go through to bring a company public.

Underwriter's Discount   The difference between the price the lead underwriter and syndicate members pay for the initial shares and the price at which they resell those shares to the institutional and individual investors. Also known as the gross spread.

Venture Capital Funding   The process of raising money for new or emerging companies. This stage takes place prior to the IPO.

index